Smithsonian Impresario

A memoir by
James Morris

When enough time has passed, events blur, facts fade and memories overtake reality. What we remember most vividly becomes for each of us our vision of the truth. We recall not the detail of an experience, but its essence—some image or moment or scrap of conversation that we think discloses meaning, captures how it was. These recollections get enshrined indelibly as anecdote and case history, dramatized in retelling as if our past lives were slide shows, either tragic or comic depending on the particular episode recalled and our current point of view. Memories filter out subtlety, shading, complexity. They distort and over- simplify. But they can also convey a special accuracy. It is just because we discriminate in our remembrances between the incidental and the essential that what we choose to recall illuminates our most profound experiences and our truest feelings.

Richard H. Pells;
The Liberal Mind in our
Conservative Age

CONTENTS

ACKNOWLEDGMENTS

I owe a special thanks to Elsie Freeman Finch for her advice & editing.

Prologue

Fall 1966

What distinguished the day from any other was the unanticipated phone call.

For months I had been prospecting for a career change in the way one does in Washington D.C.–networking, contacting people I knew or had met or had worked with– interviewing officials at various agencies. I was waiting for a response – trying not to anticipate–trained to waiting by all the auditions and readings and interviews; used to waiting for a cue, or waiting for time to enter, to play, to participate. Then the phone rang.

Charles Blitzer was calling. He had been one of my interviewers. A thin, cigarette smoking academic and classics scholar, he was Director of Education at the Smithsonian Institution (and later Assistant Secretary of Art and History.) He had been polite, very polite.

Now Blitzer told me about a meeting of the Institution's executive staff. S. Dillon Ripley, then in his second year as Smithsonian Secretary, turned the discussion to a familiar subject–his frustrated desire to 'liven up' the 120-year-old

Institution. Special events, music performances, celebrations and other programs had been discussed, but there had been no action. Blitzer said Ripley then suggested that a new person be hired, an entrepreneur or impresario–someone with experience in organizing and producing performances and other events. "The reason for my call," Blitzer said, "is to ask if you would be interested in such a position."

I was astounded! Our previous meetings had not prepared me for this invitation. It was a moment before I responded, a moment needed to regain composure. Then I said something like "Of course I need to know more, but generally I am interested." We agreed to meet.

I remembered news stories where Ripley described the Smithsonian museums as "staid and stodgy" and the National Mall as "Forest Lawn on the Potomac." In one story he spoke about museum visits as living experiences and of knowledge and learning communicated through a variety of sensory discoveries. Exciting thoughts!

In our phone conversation Blitzer had used the term 'impresario.' For someone with my career experiences the term had resonance. My mind went to the famous impresarios – Florenz Ziegfeld, P. T. Barnum, Sol Hurok – personalities I didn't associate with the Smithsonian. How would an impresario fit in with historians and scientists and researchers?

Reflecting on the path leading to this moment, it seemed labyrinthine and torturous. Two years earlier–after many years as a singer, actor, director and producer–I had put aside hopes of a career in the arts, put aside dreams of the concert stage, the theater, the opera house. Jobs in politics and producing international trade exhibitions for the U. S. Department of Commerce brought me to Washington. The life change – from artist to government employee–had been wrenching and unsatisfying. I was searching for alternatives.

♩♩♩

I had been looking for work that might bring some joy, for work that would allow me to use my library of experiences. I had talked with many people, including Senator Claiborne Pell, who was writing legislation to establish a National Endowment for the Arts and Humanities. Pell sent me to talk with his legislative assistant, Livingston Biddle.

"My friends call me "Liv," were the first words spoken when I entered Biddle's office. I had heard persistent reports – some rumors, some real – about Pell's plans for the government to support the arts through a National Foundation. Biddle was the principal author of that legislation.

I remember Liv Biddle as a warm and likable man, the independently wealthy son of a Pennsylvania family that traced its roots to colonial times. He was the author of two best-selling novels, and a Princeton University classmate of Senator Pell. Talking with him was like talking with an old friend. He studied my resume, asked many questions, and smiled. "You've had a very eclectic background" he said, "You've worked closely with a lot of talented people, performed a great deal–Juilliard, Broadway, Europe –politics. Why did you come to see me?"

I wanted to be direct, not slick, and said, "I'm enthusiastic about the idea of public support for the arts and humanities and I want to work to make that happen."

Biddle told me the details of the organization he envisioned and said, "I doubt there are many people in the Washington bureaucracy with your kind of experience. There may be a job for you. I think you should talk with Dillon Ripley, who'll chair the Federal Council on the Arts. I'll call him."

A few days later, Ripley's office responded and arranged an interview. Sidney Dillon Ripley was a New Englander, a graduate of Yale and Harvard, a noted ornithologist and author of several books on the birds of Asia. His grandfather had been president of the Union Pacific Railroad. During World War II he joined the Office of Strategic Services, the precursor of the Central Intelligence Agency. As head of intelligence services in Southeast Asia, he had trained numerous Indonesian spies. Before his appointment as Secretary of the Smithsonian, he had been Director of the Peabody Museum at Yale.

On the day of my appointment I went to Ripley's office in the original Smithsonian building, known as 'The Castle' because of its towers and minarets and battlements. The Castle appellation was emblematic. There was a sense of old-world power about the place, a style and manner that challenged those who entered. The building suited its principal occupant, for Ripley was the product of an upper-class family, a patrician who brought a sense of privilege to his relationships, a characteristic that extended to his management of the Smithsonian.

The Secretary's offices were on the second floor. There was a small elevator but I chose the carpeted stairs, past a huge oil painting entitled *Western Landscape with Lakes and Mountains,* painted in 1868 by Albert Bierstadt. The picture was a grand, romantic vision of an American frontier, painted in the style of the 19th century art movement known as the Hudson River School.

The outer office was a spacious room filled with elegant Victorian period furniture and large plants in elaborate jardinieres. Two women who appeared to be secretaries or personal assistants sat at decorative period desks.

I was shown to a chair and invited to wait. One of the women spoke with a British accent; the other, a bit younger, spoke with Bostonian inflections. A tallcase clock ticked in the stillness, and later I heard it play Westminster chimes. The scene was perfect, and I imagined directing a film shoot in this location—perhaps a scene from Henry James— *Portrait of a Lady* or W*ashington Square.*

When Ripley appeared, I saw a tall, balding man with a prominent nose. I thought he could be cast in my imaginary film scene. He said, "I have a few short stops about town. Let's talk as we drive."

His automobile was a dark-green limousine, an exception to the fleet of black vehicles that transported other government officials about the Capital. The driver was a stout black man dressed in grey chauffeur's livery. We stopped at the Riggs Bank, then at a downtown office building. Between stops, Ripley studied my resume and asked questions about my personal background, about Juilliard and about Broadways shows. He mentioned that Fred Astaire had been a family house guest. Returning to The Castle, he said plans for the staffing of the Federal Council were "up in the air." Our talk ended with vague references to further discussions.

Later, as I thought about Blitzer's call, about Ripley's statements on the Smithsonian, about my traveling interview, I questioned how an impresario might function in that environment. The Institution was founded in 1848, with a broad—and vague—mandate calling for laboratory and museum research in the arts, humanities and sciences. But an *impresario?* In Smithsonian history there had never been such a position. What sort of assignments would I be given, and what opportunities?

Liv Biddle had mentioned my "range of experiences." How would those experiences play in that society? In the chaotic political culture of Washington?

♭♭♭

In 1964 I had joined the staff of the Democratic National Committee and was assigned to the Young Democrats, where I organized entertainment and wrote speeches for vice presidential candidate Hubert Humphrey. When Humphrey was invited to speak to the Democratic Party convention in Atlantic City, he carried my best speech to the dais. He was given a riotous reception. Excited, he never looked at the speech, never glanced at the teleprompter. Instead he seemed pre-recorded, falling into a pattern of sloganeering, drawing on old campaign applause generators and improvising. He was well practiced, and the crowd loved him. Afterwards he called me to his side, thanked me for the unused speech I had slaved over and said, "Great job, Jim. Great job!"

James Morris & Vice President Huburt Humphrey

The New York Times
Published: September 30, 1964
Copyright © The New York Times

DEMOCRATS PLAN REVUE FOR VOTES

90-Minute Production Aided by Theater Professionals

By LOUIS CALTA

The Democrats, who may not be angels to everybody, will be "angels" of a Broadway type of revue this fall in a novel attempt to get out the vote, mostly on the Johnson line.

The 90-minute show, called "The Young Dem Bandwagon," has been put together by some of the theater's top-notch professionals. It was commissioned by Jim Morris, director of special activities of the Democratic National Committees.

Some of the theater's leading songwriters who have contributed material, are Harold Rome, Burton Lane, E. Y. Harburg, Betty Comden, Adolph Green and Carolyn Leigh.

Among the artists who have agreed to make limited guest appearances are Hal March, Eydie Gorme, Earl Wrightson, Peter Paul and Mary, Lois Hunt, Mary Blyden, Judy Collins, Kitty Kallen and Odetta.

"The Young Dem Bandwagon" will open with a number called "Politics Tonight." It is a takeoff on the song "Comedy Tonight" from "A Funny Thing Hapened on the Way to the Forum."

It goes:

Drop what you're doin'
Something is brewin'
Fellow belligerents
It's politics tonight.

We've got the goods
We've got the slate
Out where the vote is
Let's circulate.

Louis Calta article, NY Times, 9/30/64

In a later experience I commissioned a 90-minute, get-out-the-vote music revue, *The Young Dem Bandwagon*. Stone Widney, production head for lyricist Alan Jay Lerner, produced it, the theater's leading songwriters contributed material, and stars such as Eydie Gorme, Peter, Paul and Mary and Judy Collins agreed to limited guest appearances.

The Bandwagon opened in Columbus, Ohio, and starred Peter Boyle, Ina Balin and comic Shelley Berman. The Democratic Committee in Washington inserted appearances by Ambassador John Kenneth Galbraith and the President's teenaged daughter Lucy Johnson. Galbraith talked for more than an hour, Lucy Johnson was incoherent, the audience twitched and fretted, Berman fumed and *The Bandwagon* became an exercise in anarchy and confusion. Berman gave me a piercing look and stormed out the theater's rear door. I followed him. He ran up the stage door alley and I ran after him. Before he reached the street I caught him, turned him around and urged him to return to the rally. He responded with an out-pouring of obscenities. .I didn't have time to argue. I grasped his coat collar, dragging him up the alley, into the stage door and across the backstage area. If his alley obscenities were blue, his back stage obscenities were purple. Galbraith finished his speech and I gave Berman a shove onto the stage. The audience must have thought the action was planned, and they began a prolonged applause. Berman straightened his coat, smiled at the audience, and glared at me, standing in the wings. Then he walked to the microphone and said, "Thank you Ambassador, thank you for warming up the audience." Applause. Then he began his act, and the audience laughed.

Nothing cures the wounds of an actor like applause. Nothing placates a comic like a laugh. Berman finished his act and exited. As he walked by me he muttered something about charging me with abuse. He departed on the morning plane and we haven't spoken since.   Did the show add votes to the Democratic Party column in the election? I have no way of knowing - but President Johnson won in a landslide.

After these experiences I had no enthusiasm for politics. My thoughts turned instead to my family and my mentors, the teachers and artists and professionals who had shaped my world-view and my understanding of culture, those denizens who nurtured creative inspirations and did not live in castles. So the past had been an overture, and the show begins with memories

ONE

The Domain

November 1966. I joined the Smithsonian staff, temporarily occupying an existing position as Director of Museum Services. Within a few months a new office was created, a Division of Performing Arts, and I was installed as its director.

I had worked in many places, but never in a castle. I was given a pleasant office on the second floor, with antique furniture, a secretary and a view of the Mall. I was down the hall from Secretary Ripley, near Under Secretary Jim Bradley and across from Assistant Secretary for Science Sidney Galler. General Counsel Peter Powers, Charles Blitzer, and Academic Programs Director Philip Ritterbush were around the corner. I was given no job description and no mission statement.

With the exception of Bradley, this group and others on the senior management team known as 'the secretariat' reflected the style of the boss. They were all white males, all products of Eastern style and privilege, all ivy-league alumnae. The clothing was mostly by Brooks Brothers or J. Press, the shoes by Johnston and Murphy, the neckties regimental stripes or small dots against a solid background, the cigarettes were Players or Benson and Hedges.

I never heard anyone use the word 'class,' as in upper class or middle class, but in commenting on a new hire I heard Ripley ask, "Is he clubbable?"

Growing up, I had developed a strong, negative reaction to attempts at class identification. Of course I was aware of social classes—no one raised in the South could escape them. But I was also aware of the damaging bigotry and racism that often followed such categorization.

Jim Bradley had a different style. He was a career government executive, smooth and practiced in the bureaucratic arts. He treated me kindly and suggested that I spend some time getting acquainted with the domain. Dr. Galler, a biologist and environmentalist, was distant but friendly. Peter Powers, the Smithsonian's first General Counsel, attended the Groton School, Oxford University and Harvard Law School, and was interested in music. His manner was amiable, if slightly patronizing. Dr. Ritterbush was a historian of science; young and sharp. Dr. Charles Blitzer had been my initial Smithsonian contact. He was a graduate of Harvard and former president of the Phi Beta Kappa Society. He was very pleasant and invited me to join everyone at afternoon tea. In the past I hadn't taken to the British tea ritual, despite spending a year in a theater company of tea-drinkers, but it seemed to be a good idea to accept Blitzer's invitation.

The following day was beautiful, with the trees on the Mall dropping the last of their leaves. I decided to take a walk and sort through my impressions. In the past I had frequently walked the halls of the Smithsonian museums and enjoyed many of the exhibitions. Now I searched the exhibitions, looking for a deeper understanding of the ideas behind the displays.

The National Museum of Natural History was a great research facility with collections that included millions of science specimens and cultural artifacts. I saw a huge stuffed elephant dominating the foyer. In the halls were exhibits of insects, marine and plant life and specimens showing the origins of human life. There were the bones of dinosaurs and American Indian artifacts, displays of African ethnology and the Hope Diamond and more. The vast museum had traditionally been very popular with visitors. I remembered Ripley saying, "Stuffed animals, glass cases full of curiosities, replicas, models, facsimiles. But the natural world is full of life. Our representations of that world are dead.

"𝄞𝄞𝄞

I walked through the National Museum of History and Technology (now the National Museum of American History.) Exhibitions included Edison's light bulb, Whitney's cotton gin, power machinery and engines, coins and paper currency, military objects, clocks, First Ladies gowns and President Lincoln's hat-an amazing display of Americana.

To me, the most interesting part of the museum was the Hall of Musical Instruments, an elegant room designed for occasional performances on instruments in the collection. On view were examples of rare string, wind and keyboard instruments from the 18th, 19th and 20th centuries, many in protected glass cases. The instrument collection was first organized by Assistant Secretary G. Brown Goode in 1879. Some instruments came from the 1876 Philadelphia

Centennial Exposition. Wind instruments, banjos and music boxes were donated by J. Howard Foote in 1914 with keyboards donated by Hugo Worch. In all, the collection held some 8,000 instruments. There was a schedule of demonstrations that explored the unique characteristics of the instruments, with occasional performances of baroque and classical period music.

A special temporary exhibit entitled *Music Making American Style* displayed instruments used in early brass and jazz bands. I looked at several folk instruments-mandolins, guitars, a fretless banjo and a mountain dulcimer similar to an instrument my friend Frank Proffitt made. Ripley had said, "Take those instruments from their cases and make them sing again." No one I knew used language like that.

My final visit was the Freer Gallery of Art. The collections of Asian art, including paintings, sculpture, lacquer, metalwork and ceramics, were renowned and made a stark contrast to the adjacent western art and crafts. The gallery was a gift to the United States from art collector and philanthropist Charles Lang Freer. Freer also endowed the Gallery, making it financially independent of other Smithsonian entities. At the center of the building was a beautifully landscaped courtyard with a fountain and places for visitors to rest and contemplate.

Because the Smithsonian exhibitions were so vast and numerous, my walking tour took several days. Throughout I recalled Ripley's idea that museums were 'tools for the enhancement of human knowledge, with collections that helped interpret our lives and our environment'. In my initial interview he had described an educated person as 'one who can do more than simply read with their eyes, but read with

4

their hands and ears and develop a comprehensive talent for living with their senses.'

What Ripley had *not* talked about were the conflicts that existed in the idea of a museum: the assumption of excellence and permanence that dominated collections. And most damaging of all was the image of collections as the plunder and swag of a colonial authority.

By the end of my tour, the wealth and variety of the collections, plus the scope of Ripley's vision of museums, left me with a kaleidoscope of ideas and impressions.

Adding to these impressions was a call some days later from Ripley. I was to accompany him to the White House. Lady Bird Johnson had called a meeting of executives supporting her efforts to beautify the Capital and the entire United States. We gathered in the Blue Room before a large bouquet of mixed flowers decorating a center table. As they were introduced, the executives responded with short speeches, usually beginning with "I am honored to stand before this distinguished company of..." followed by the names and titles. At his introduction, Ripley continued. "I am honored to stand before this distinguished company of....." and he called each flower in the bouquet by its botanical name.

Some of the attendees may have felt put-down, others may have thought they were victims of one-upmanship. I don't think Ripley gave much thought to what their reactions would be. Nevertheless, it was a stunning, witty performance and another example of Ripley's unique style.

Returning to my office, I found several file folders on my desk containing background information about my initial assignments. One file folder had a brief description of occasional performance programs in the Musical Instruments

5

Hall of the Museum of History and Technology. There were scribbled notes regarding expansion of these performances to include renaissance and baroque music, performed in costume, from the parapet of the Castle. It was music I loved, colorful and evocative music. But the image of a princely ensemble, evoking another time and place, another culture, seemed incongruous.

Another folder was labeled Smithsonian Son et Lumier and contained plans for a sound and light production modeled on the popular spectacles at some historic sites in Europe. At these productions, audiences saw a visual and sound reenactment of events associated with the site's history. A Smithsonian Son et Lumier would use The Castle as background for the story of James Smithson, English scientist and bastard son of the Duke of Northumberland, who willed money to the United States 'for the increase and diffusion of knowledge among men.' Congress argued about accepting the money for months before agreeing and issuing vague usage guidelines. Writer and producer John Houseman had been given $5,000 to develop a narrative script.

A third folder concerned the installation of a carousel on the Mall. The Smithsonian owned an elegant machine with animals carved by George Dentzel. Ripley admired the carousel, which reminded him of boyhood summers spent in Paris–days alternating between studies with a tutor, visits to museums, crepes bought from a vendor and rides on the carousel in the Jardin des Tuileries. "Pleasure and learning blended seamlessly together, as they should be." The Dentzel machine was stored in a suburban warehouse and required extensive renovation.

Another folder contained notes about projects such as a 'bridge of sighs,' linking Ripley's castle office with the Arts and Industries Building, the Smithsonian's second oldest museum – a fanciful Victorian edifice built to house exhibits from the 1871 Philadelphia Centennial Exhibition. Another folder mentioned the development of a self-destructing beer bottle that would reduce the glut of waste products. Neither of these ideas enjoyed serious consideration.

A final folder contained correspondence about a national college drama festival, an idea promoted by actress Peggy Wood. In talks with Wood, Ripley had endorsed the idea. Because the Smithsonian had no theater, or appropriate space, he suggested erecting a tent theater on the Mall.

Later, in talks with Jim Bradley, I was told there was no money in the Smithsonian budget for any of these projects.

Faced with Bradley's news, I wondered what the hell I had gotten into, what to do. Ripley couldn't provide any answers, he had left Washington to spend time at his estate in Litchfield, Connecticut, and essential correspondence was sent to him by daily messenger. So I decided to read Houseman's draft script.

I was disappointed. I thought Houseman's work was lacking in drama and imagination. When Houseman asked my opinion, I chickened out and changed the subject. I didn't know Ripley or Houseman very well, I heard Ripley refer to Houseman as "Jack," and assumed there was a relationship of some kind. I knew he was impressed with Jack's name-dropping and I didn't intend to be set up at this early point in my association.

In the 1930s and '40s Houseman had collaborated with Orson Welles in the depression era Federal Theater Project. And he co-produced Welles' classic film, *Citizen Kane*. (Houseman said he and Joseph Mankiewicz wrote the screenplay, a claim that Welles hotly disputed, leading to a

7

break in their relationship that was never repaired.) The enterprising Houseman rebounded by producing other films, including *Executive Suite, Blue Dahlia, They Live By Night, This Property Is Condemned* and a version of *Shakespeare's Julius Caesar*. The later has a very nuanced performance of Mark Antony by Marlon Brando that's worth study.

Houseman had a personal quality often referred to as "gravitas." The "gravitas" image received its due in a Robin Williams satire, where he played a Houseman reading the phone book. He was very funny. The 'gravitas' was mostly a façade, but it helped him obtain an acting role in the popular film, *The Paper Chase*. He also made television commercials, as in "We make money the old fashioned way – we earn it" for the brokerage firm Smith Barney.

In 1966 Houseman was down on his luck and grateful for the Smithsonian contract. When he again asked for my opinion about his script, I told him. He smiled an enigmatic smile.

Later I learned that he had never liked the Smithsonian story as the subject for a sound and light production. "Too much talk and not enough action" was his assessment. More to his taste was the Son et Lumier production at Versailles, set on the eve of the French revolution, with fountains aglow and a large cast of costumed actors and lopped off heads rolling on the cobblestones.

I made cuts from Houseman's script, and with a few production drawings, I assembled a brief fund raising proposal. Ripley returned from Connecticut, approved the proposal, and we made some fund-raising presentations, where we were met with blank stares and no commitments. Ripley didn't give up easily. He authorized $7,000 for an electrical feasibility study, but that failed to make the project more attractive to funding sources. I hoped Ripley's interest would wane. In time it did.

For the carousel project, Ripley had asked noted designer and architect Charles Eames for a plan to house the Dentzel on the Mall. My office had been moved to the 19th century Arts and Industry building, and Eames was working on an exhibition in an adjacent gallery. He frequently stopped by to use the telephone and to chat. He was warm and amiable, easy to talk with. He learned I had worked in the theater and shared some of his experiences as a set designer. He talked about the importance of connections between people of different backgrounds and experiences, and he showed me sketches for a marvelous beveled glass carousel enclosure, with glass panels suspended to catch the revolving carousel's colored lights. It would be a piece of glistening kinetic sculpture, a jewel on the Mall.

Preliminary cost estimates came to more than a million dollars. More detailed estimates passed $20 million and Ripley's interest faded.

As an alternative, I found a man named Jim Wells who collected carousels and antique popcorn wagons. Wells agreed to provide a good carousel and to manage its operation. I also found an antique band organ that played typical carousel music. With careful management, the carousel showed a small, consistent profit. Ripley was delighted, and this arrangement was still in operation when I retired almost 20 years later.

At the same time, I was meeting with several people concerning the American College Theater Festival.

The idea for a festival to recognize and encourage college and university theater programs originated with the

American Educational Theater Association. Because of her life-long interest in training American actors and directors, actress Peggy Wood became an early and active advocate. Ms. Wood approached the Smithsonian and the soon-to-be-opened Kennedy Canter for the Performing Arts. Both Ripley and Kennedy Center President Roger Stevens pledged their support.

I think it was impossible not to like Peggy Wood. In 1966 she was 75 years old and in the twilight of a great career. She was also a charmer. She had recently been nominated for an Academy Award as best supporting actress in the motion picture version of *The Sound of Music*. She had made her Broadway debut in 1917 and had a long, successful stage career, but she was most remembered as Mama in the hit television series *I Remember Mama* that ran for seven years and earned her millions of fans.

As we worked with the American Educational Theater Association to organize the festival, Peggy became a close friend. Together we sought support from members of Congress, corporations and private donors. At last, in 1969 the first American College Theater Festival was launched, with performances at Ford's Theater and a tent theater on the Mall. The festival continues today, now sponsored in part by the U. S. Department of Education. Every year the festival involves hundreds of theater programs nationwide and more than 18,000 participants.

TWO

Reflections

Early 1967 and my initial assignments were on the shelf or moving slowly forward. I felt good about my management of the portfolio of enlivening ideas. So did Ripley, Blitzer and other members of the 'secretariat.' I had been so engrossed in performing successfully in my new job that I had not found time to reconnoiter. Now I began to assimilate, to re-acquaint myself with the museums, the city and the buildings on the Mall, and to digest an accumulation of impressions and sensations.

I wanted to become more familiar with the arts scene in Washington and gratefully accepted a lunch invitation from Patrick Hayes, head of the Washington Performing Arts Society. Following lunch we walked to Constitution Hall. That evening Hayes was presenting Arthur Rubinstein in concert, and the famous pianist was on the stage, giving his recently tuned piano a thorough workout. We stood and chatted for several minutes until Rubinstein asked us to leave so he could practice.

"I can't practice if anyone is listening," he said. "If the cat is in the room, I'll perform for the cat! That's not practicing."

We smiled and said our good-byes to Mr. Rubinstein, and that evening I returned to Constitution Hall as a member of the audience. It was a stunning performance by a great artist, and the audience loved him. I wondered if there was a role for great virtuosos in the Hall of Musical Instruments programs.

At this time, the National Council on the Arts was meeting to award its initial round of grants. The Council was appointed to make policy for the National Endowment. Roger Stevens was the chairman, and Council members, including Ripley, were appointed by President Johnson. For this meeting, Ripley was otherwise involved and appointed me his surrogate.

Council meetings were entertaining and fun to watch. More than a dozen nationally known artists and philanthropists had been appointed. They had money to dispense, and everyone wanted to be heard. I was reminded of an orchestra tuning up, a cacophony of horns and winds playing melodies and egocentric tunes. Stevens was used to making decisions–after all, he was the man who purchased the Empire State Building on a weekend-and he moved quickly through the agenda, managing the process with a deft hand.

As I watched Stevens, I was also comparing him to Ripley. Earlier I had been invited to a small dinner party at Ripley's home where Stevens was also a guest. He seemed uncomfortable with small talk. He was not very polished in social situations, and whatever the subject, his response was usually direct and straightforward. I thought he was very different from the urbane Ripley.

So I gained some distance from carousels and sound and light productions and was able to open my imagination to the possibilities of a performing arts enterprise in a museum.

I found real enthusiasm for the Division of Musical Instruments performances. I thought perhaps we should make use of existing enlivenment resources before creating new programs. It concerned me somewhat that the best instruments in the collection dictated a concentration on baroque and classical period music when the museum was about American history and culture. I was familiar with the repertory. I had been a soloist at St. Paul's Chapel at Columbia University, and at other New York churches and sang the bass solos in Haydn's *Lord Nelson Mass* and *The Creation,* in Bach's *B Minor Mass,* in Handel's *Messiah, in Verdi's Requiem* and similar works. Most of all, I liked the use of the instrument collection as a base for music programming. I temporarily shelved my worries that such a focus would marginalize the powerful story of American music.

James Weaver was in charge of performances. Jim was an excellent harpsichordist, enthusiastic and knowledgeable. The content of his programs didn't need my input; they needed instead an advocate and a fundraiser – and maybe a push in the direction of hiring top-flight musicians. Maybe Jim hired too many academics?

The Musical Instrument Division's small staff struggled to restore and maintain instruments in the collections, and they were not well funded. The work required trained artisans and it was expensive and time consuming. The great quality and depth of the collections was not widely known. Could a strong musical advocate bring better visibility? Would broader programming raise the visibility and attract donors and new acquisitions? Certainly programming should include folk and popular music. Perhaps there could be an orchestra of professional soloists, with members able to work in any configuration and make full use of the collection? It was a cause worth time, effort and passion.

I had brought my folk festival experience with me. Now I saw evidence of a robust American folk culture visible in many parts of the museum collections. I thought a Smithsonian folk festival would enliven the collections and be a central focus of a re-invigorated National Mall. A festival could also cross racial, class and social boundaries.

During my survey of the History and Technology Museum, I had been surprised at the absence of any object or material, any photo display, any label, that mentioned the presence or contributions of African-Americans. Nor did I see any mention of other minority cultures as part of American society. Whenever there was an opportunity I pushed the subject of racial imbalance in Smithsonian priorities. I could sense the discomfort that my pushing caused.

Ripley finally responded and addressed this problem for the first time in his 1970 Smithsonian Year Report. "Historical museums tend to become fossilized. Entrance into these 'cemeteries' is considered by historians not only a bore but a trial. Far too little has been done to delineate the history of ethnic minorities of our country or to single out and describe their achievement. As a result, our ethnic subcultures, our minority groups, come off very badly indeed."

14

I had met the museum directors, most of the bureau heads and administrative staff. They were intelligent people, experts in their chosen fields and for the most part warm and friendly. It would have been unthinkable to cast any of them as racists or bigots, but I could not put aside the idea that I was staring at a form of institutional racism and that froze me in my tracks. Was a performing arts outfit intended as a solution to unspoken racial problems and attitudes? Nothing of the kind had been mentioned. Was I supposed to create programs that would address major institutional social needs? If so, why was I not told if social and cultural problems were a root cause for my hiring?

I took a walk. Could a folk festival be the device for reaching groups and communities often ignored by museums?

As for American popular culture, the subject also caused discomfort. Perhaps it was too ubiquitous, omnipresent and prominent to be ignored, and too powerful to be passed over. American popular culture had also become a force in world culture, but the museum world had been slow to embrace popular culture programs, perhaps a result of long-established snobbery.

Popular culture had also been an anathema to the academic establishment, but attitudes were changing. I agreed with recent comments by archivist and editor, Elsie Freeman Finch, when she said, "My theory about snobbery and pop culture? It seems to me that those who view advocates of popular culture as somehow beneath them allow so-called elites to maintain class structure. We educated, you not. We sensitive, you a thug, and so on. But in reality, we

15

now know that a lot of popular culture reflects social realities."

I was reasonably sure that this was not the sort of enlivenment Secretary Ripley originally had in mind when I was hired. Yet to ignore popular culture would advertise that the Smithsonian was indeed "the nations attic, remote, out-of-touch and archaic." But we could make a start. We could embrace popular music, with its roots in Tin-Pan Alley, ragtime and blues, folk songs and rock and roll. And we could embrace American musical theater, with its popular entertainment history, its roots in European opera and operetta and its appeal to the mainstream. Perhaps we could present jazz music, something I had wanted to program from the outset. I believed jazz, with its roots in the folk community and its development into an accepted art form, had entered the pantheon.

As for the collections of American, Asian and eastern art, I thought the museum's ethnographic exhibitions also lacked a feeling of life. A visitor could stand and study the material culture objects on display in exhibitions, but it was hard to image human hands using the objects. The collection presented opportunities to program visiting foreign music, dance and theater ensembles.

And finally there were the numerous forms of cultural expression that overwhelmed established categories. These included the changing and challenging sounds of contemporary music, the non-verbal communication of modern American dance, the direct contact of audience and artists in performance art and experimental theater, plus popular film and television productions.

16

Was this list of opportunities too ambitious, too all-inclusive? Possibly. I became a student with an eye and ear open to my new environment and the daily developments in American culture.

Where to begin? The Performing Arts Division was the new child in the Smithsonian family and needed a success to signal our arrival. I thought the best choice would be folk culture.

THREE

Paul Green and the American Folk Festival

Remember the folk song revival, that era of commercial successful folk music? Media focus was centered on the boom in popular recordings of new and old folk songs and on public events such as the Newport Folk Festival and the Philadelphia Folk Festival. Woody Guthrie, Pete Seeger, Jimmie Rodgers, Burl Ives, Harry Belafonte and such groups as The Weavers, The Kingston Trio and the Limelighters. Joan Baez, Bob Dylan, Phil Ochs, Tom Paxton and others were part of it. And don't forget a million guitar-strumming kids who copied what they heard on recordings and in performances.

But what about the real 'folk,' the people whose music fueled the boom? They were invoked in *Sing Out!* magazine, acknowledged from the stage and romanticized in the press, but they usually didn't share in the money.

I was living and working in Germany when I became interested in American folk music, and I wanted to know more about 'the folk' that produced it. I saw a lot of exploitation happening, so I looked for writers and scholars who cared about 'the folk,' who cared about people. On the library shelf, I found some work by Paul Green.

Green was recognized as one of America's most distinguished writers. The first American playwright from the South to achieve national and international recognition, he was among the first to speak out in favor of human rights and against war. He also opposed the death penalty and decried the devastating effects of racism and poverty on common people. Paul also understood exploitation.

We met face-to-face in 1958, and through his acquaintance I came to understand more about the richness of America's folk culture and the broader social context of which it was a part. In many ways, Paul had a profound influence on my subsequent life and work.

Paul had studied philosophy at the University of North Carolina before turning to writing. His play, *In Abraham's Bosom*, was a ground-breaking depiction of African-American life in the South, and it earned him the Pulitzer Prize for Drama in 1927. Another play, *The House of Connelly*, launched the seminal Group Theater and is often compared to Chekhov's *The Cherry Orchard*.

Unhappy with commercial theater, Paul returned to North Carolina. In 1932 he was lured to Hollywood where in a two-year period he wrote award-winning vehicles for Will Rogers and George Arliss, two major stars of early films.

Paul had a favorite story about his association with Rogers, the American cowboy, comedian, humorist and once Hollywood's top-paid star. At the studio, Paul was assigned an office located far from other writers and removed from producers and executives. The location was chosen to isolate him from Rogers, who executives characterized as "difficult, ornery and impossible to work with."

"The son-of-a-bitch won't like anything you write," Green was told. Rogers knew how he was regarded, and despite the precautions, he located Paul in his back lot retreat. They hit it off and thereafter met in secret. They talked about the story, the characters and the developing script. At the pre-production meeting, with anxious producers and executives anticipating the star's total rejection of the script, everyone was amazed as Rogers leapt to his feet, praised the writing and announced his complete approval of all production plans.

The film, *State Fair*, was a huge commercial success and won Paul an Oscar for best screen play. Years later he won a second Oscar–shared with Oscar Hammerstein-for a musical version of the story. In addition to the Pulitzer and the Oscars,' Green won two Guggenheim Fellowships and honorary doctorates from seven major universities. He remains an integral part of a Southern writer's renaissance that includes William Faulkner, Thomas Wolfe, Katherine Ann Porter, Alan Tate, Robert Penn Warren and others.

From 1934 to 1945 Paul served as president of the National Folk Festival Association. Ben Bodkin, Zora Neale Hurston, Constance Rourke, George Pullen Jackson, Arthur Campa, George Korson, Richard Dorson, J. Frank Dobie and Bascom Lunsford, all well known names in academic circles, were also Board members. Eleanor Roosevelt was an active supporter and honorary chairman of the Association. A National Festival was presented each year in a different city. Each board member recommended participants. Otherwise the selection of participants was rather enigmatic and included traditional artists and aspiring performers who sang folk songs.

When we met, Paul was working on a new musical play about Stephen Foster, America's first great song writer. I had been invited to audition for the leading role.

Over lunch he described his new play, then talk drifted to his folk festival experiences. We talked about cultural roots and the festival idea. We listened to recordings of fiddlers, a Cajun band, a polka band, to Horton Barker, Texas Gladden and Hobart Smith, and I was hooked. I heard performers with great musical skills playing music that was free of artifice, music that grew from family and community traditions. The performances were skillful but absent the commercial patina of the uptown bars, clubs and concert halls — performances that relied instead on an unselfconscious vigor and personal involvement.

Throughout our talks, Paul reiterated his belief that folk festivals must be vehicles for affirmation, not sources of profit. That sounded right to me.

After lunch I sang some of Stephen Foster's songs. Paul listened intently, but he was restless, walking about the room as if searching for some lost article. I think auditions made him nervous. He was a big man with large hands. He had been raised in the country, a farm boy and small-town baseball player grown to regional poet.

Isaac Van Grove was arranging Foster's songs for the stage production, and he was a lovely musician. His arrangements seemed so natural, the melodic lines flowing effortlessly, and the harmonies adding a subtle richness to Foster's compositions.

Paul's play was entitled *The Stephen Foster Story* and it followed his idea of a 'symphonic drama,' combining music, text and pageantry to tell a historic story. It was a concept first used in *The Lost Colony*, a production that had been playing in Manteo, North Carolina since the 1930s. The Foster show was to play at a new theater in My Old Kentucky Home State Park in Bardstown, Kentucky.

I returned home, still thinking more about folk festivals than Stephen Foster. A few days later the Stephen Foster producer called and offered me the title role.

As I thought about the offer, my mind flashed back to my two-year sojourn in Germany, where I had gone to gain experience as an opera singer. I had a scrapbook full of good critical reviews for work as a concert singer and stage director, but German theaters cast me mostly in American operas, not the core operatic repertory I desired.

And in Germany, my son, James Morris III, was born. I remain very proud of the man that he has become.

The two years in Germany had been a growth time. It began when I sang for Albert Mohr, a major agent for theater and operatic talent. Mohr liked my voice and agreed to represent me. We determined that my 'fach'– the German system of typecasting – was lyrischer bariton, or spielbariton, specializing in the Mozart and Italian operatic repertory.

It was winter, past the hiring season for most German theaters, but there was an opening in Regensburg, a small city near the Czech border. I had purchased a used automobile, an English-made Morris Minor, and set out to audition for the Intendant (General Manager) and Chief Conductor. They asked me to sing a Papageno aria from Mozart's *The Magic Flute*, Germont's aria from Verdi's *La Traviata*, and Renato's aria from Verdi's *The Masked Ball*. I sang well, and I liked the charming theater on the banks of the Danube River. Their response was very positive and they promised a decision in a short time.

I returned to Frankfurt and shortly received a letter from the Regensburg Intendant telling me they had decided to hire an older German singer. I was depressed by the news. And I was running out of money.

I applied for a job conducting the Frankfurt German/American Chorus. My Juilliard experiences with Robert Shaw impressed the organizations managers and I was hired, for a small weekly fee. A few months later I was also hired as music director at the Frankfurt Playhouse, the oldest established English language theater in Europe.

James Morris, Music Director, Frankfurt Playhouse, 1957

With the two jobs I was making enough to live and pay the rent on our apartment.

I began my Playhouse tenure with a concert of American songs, sponsored by Amerika Haus, the United States Information Agency's Cultural Center and Library in Frankfurt. At their request I programmed American music. I was accompanied by American pianist Hugh McGinnis, who wrote two new songs for me to sing.

I knew the concert would be a major opportunity. I wanted the song selection to make a strong impression, and remembered when I sang on several recordings of music composed by Pulitzer Prize winner Henry Brant. It was Henry who introduced me to the music of Charles Ives, and together we analyzed and deconstructed some of Ives innovative songs. It was a revelation. I thought they were idiomatically the most truly American songs I had ever heard.

For the Frankfurt concert Hugh and I programmed several Ives pieces. He played a movement from the *Concord Sonata* and I sang a group of songs, ending with Ives setting of Vachel Lindsay's poem, *General William Booth Enters Into Heaven*. The text evoked scenes of men driven mad by degradation, sex, alcohol, narcotics, and despair, finally to be saved and ushered into heaven by General Booth, the founder of the Salvation Army. The song is very atonal and poly-rhythmic, infused with shouts and screams of anguish. It was also hard as hell to perform. The piano accompaniment calls for fists pounding the keys in simulated drum effects, then cacophonic smears as forearms push across the keyboard. Woven through the noise are bits of hymn tunes and popular ditties. According to Lindsay's directions, a performance of the song should be acted as well as sung. The audience was shocked, then amused, and then they exploded with enthusiastic response.

The concert was very successful. German music critics particularly liked the Ives compositions with their evocations of Americana. The critic for the Frankfurter Rundschau wrote "Two young Americans appeared before a German American audience, to much applause. The baritone, James Morris, with his beautiful performance, sang with great art and expression."

As a result of the Frankfurt concert I became strongly identified with American music. Hugh and I repeated our program in numerous other German cities. We added selections of German classical lieder and continued to receive concert offers for months. There were also guest artist contracts for performances in several German opera houses, but the contracts were mainly for American musicals and operas, including Lerner and Loewe's *Brigadoon*; Frank Loesser's *The Most Happy Fella*; Gian Carlo Menotti's *Amahl and the Night Visitors*; Leonard Bernstein's *Trouble in Tahiti* and Kurt Weill's *Down in the Valley*. There were also offers for me to stage some of these works.

Altogether I was now making good money, but my earnings were sporadic. The lack of continuing security affected my family life and my wife was having periods of depression. I had come to Germany seeking an operatic career, but despite Albert Mohr's reassurances, no resident opera company offered me a long-term contract.

Responding to the strong public enthusiasm for the concert programs, Amerika Haus asked me to do another concert. I wanted to establish a different musical profile, so I sang Dietrich Buxtehude's Cantata #8, *Mein Herz ist Bereit*, with string quartet and piano, Samual Barber's *Dover Beach*, with string quartet and a Mozart concert aria from *Cosi fan Tutti*. The Rundshau critic wrote that my singing was "a bit dry" in the Buxtehude, but in the Mozart I was "in my element." But at the end of the review I was still identified with American songs and operas.

27

Then an anomaly occurred. The German public broadcaster Hessischer Rundfunk approached Amerika Haus about a series of programs exploring American popular songs. The Rundfunk producers wanted to find an expert program consultant, and the Amerika Haus staff recommended me. That recommendation thrust me into meaningful work, and a new assessment of my resources.

The Amerika Haus library had enough reference books, and I remembered intense conversations with Bill Engvick, Joe Moon and others about the compositional quality of many popular songs. Indeed, Bill had written memorable lyrics to several Alec Wilder songs. Over the years, I had been drilled in song analysis by various teachers and coaches. Frequently, when others wrote about music, I had been put off by obscure language and academic jargon, by forced metaphors and unclear descriptions. I didn't know whether I could do any better, but I was moved to try.

Writing about American popular songs, I tried to avoid the traps and explain clearly why I thought the songs merited inclusion in the canon of great song writing. I responded to the Rundfunk's request with a narrative script that was translated into German and aired several times.

Among the American songs I selected were *I'm Beginning To See the Light* (Duke Ellington, Johnny Hodges and Harry James); *Say It Isn't So, Isn't This a Lovely Day*, and *I t Only Happens When I Dance With You* (Irving Berlin); *I Get A Kick Out Of You, Night and Day* and *In The Still Of The Night* (Cole Porter)*; Haunted Heart* (Howard Dietz and Arthur Schwartz;) *Come Rain or Come Shine* and *Ac-cen-tchu-Ate the Positive* (Johnny Mercer and Harold Arlen.)

Shortly after I submitted my American Popular Song copy to the Hessischer Rundfunk I received a phone call from Joe Moon, acting as my agent. I had been offered a high-paying concert booking in Flint, Michigan. It was then that I was asked to audition for Paul Green's new musical play. Acting on this news, Joe had submitted my audio tape to NBC-TV's *Today Show*, and I was booked to appear on the show.

**James Morris, guest artist, The Today Show,
NBC-TV w/audience member**

With the concert income, an offer from the Stephen Foster producer, and the national prominence of the *Today* show, I decided to make a visit home.

There were sleepless nights. The pressure of family obligations weighed heavily. Accepting the Stephen Foster role would mean a permanent return to the United States and likely an end to my operatic ambitions. It was a difficult decision, made more so by a call from Albert Mohr, my German opera agent, reporting that I had been offered a full time contract by a good company, with assignments spanning the entire operatic repertory. It was a good opportunity , but first-year pay would be small. It was a painful choice, but finally I decided to decline the contract and stay in the United States. My wife and son joined me, and a few weeks later we moved to Bardstown to begin pre-production promotional work for Paul Green's show.

The Stephen Foster Story opened on June 16th, 1959, and played six performances a week for 11 weeks. The press and public reaction was enthusiastic, and the show continues every summer, now enjoying one of the longest runs in American theater history. It has also been an economic boon to Bardstown.

James Morris as Stephen Foster, NY Times photo 1959

Because of *The Stephen Foster Story,* I was offered a series of concerts in Kentucky, Tennessee, Indiana and Ohio. It was enjoyable work, but it was seasonal and lacked the economic security I needed.

I returned to New York City, but concert and theater bookings brought me back to the area for some time. In 1962, while working in Asheville, North Carolina, a local official asked if I would be interested in producing their Mountain Dance and Folk Festival, an Asheville tradition since 1927. The festival was founded by Bascom Lunsford as a way for natives of the Appalachian region to know and value their cultural heritage. Now Lunsford was in bad health and the future of his festival was in doubt. I had heard about Lunsford and his festival from Paul Green, and thought the festival's demise would be a grave loss.

My interest in folk culture had grown steadily, beginning with those early discussions with Paul. He had urged me to study the work of several folklorists and cultural historians, and the continuing national popularity of folk songs had kept my interest alive. I decided to produce the Asheville festival but did not keep Lunsford's Mountain Dance and Folk Festival title in case a revival was possible. I chose instead to name the new event the American Folk Festival.

I was a performer and producer, not a folklorist. I also wanted to produce an event with real integrity, and a focus on traditional, 'real' folk performers. So I called Alan Lomax, former head of the Library of Congress Folksong Archive, and asked for his help. He was living in New York City and was deeply involved in other projects. At first he declined my request, but he did invite me to visit him and discuss my plans.

Alan was a brilliant man. The son of John Lomax, pioneering teacher and ethnomusicologist, Alan joined his father on extensive research trips and helped found the Library's Folksong Archive with its landmark collection of field recordings.

Meeting with Alan in his Greenwich Village apartment, I found a passionate person of wide intelligence and deep commitment to the study of folk culture. He also was opinionated, egotistical and cantankerous. He spent the first half hour of our meeting proclaiming his unwillingness to digress from his current research. Then he spent the next two days giving me a long list of folk musicians I must invite to Asheville. He insisted I go personally to meet as many of these artists as possible. And finally, toward the end of our extended conversations, he said he would put aside his work for a few days and come to Asheville to personally emcee the performances. My budget was limited, but it was an offer I couldn't refuse.

With Alan's list in hand, I started on a long field trip. In southern Virginia I met Hobart 'Hobe' Smith, the legendary virtuoso. Paul Green had played a recording of Hobe, who now told me he taught himself to play piano in a weekend, harmonica in a day or two and couldn't remember when he had *not* played the guitar, banjo and fiddle. Brushing aside any wisp of modesty, he said he could play any musical instrument ever made. And he could!

With Hobe's agreement to join the festival lineup, I traveled on, searching for Sanklers Creek, home of blind ballad singer Horton Barker. There was no Sanklers Creek on the map. Stopping at a sheriff's office, I learned I had been misled by an Appalachian accent and should have looked instead for Saint Clair's Creek. Barker was living with a relative, and dressed in bib overalls he stood and sang unaccompanied ballads for a hour. Soft, sweet, melodic singing.

Driving into North Carolina, I found Frank Proffitt, a mountain farmer and carpenter who made and played old-time fretless banjos and dulcimers. Frank had recorded *Tom Dooley*, a song about a local murder, and Lomax had published the song in his *Folk Songs of North America*. The Kingston Trio made a hit recording, but Frank had not been included in the royalty contract. With help from Frank Warner, a settlement was arranged and Proffitt was given a small payment.

Near Boone, North Carolina, I met a young, blind guitarist and singer named Doc Watson. I was awed by his instrumental facility and warm, unaffected singing style. He was recommended by Lomax, and he agreed to take a bus to the festival if he could be accompanied by his teenaged son, Merle.

I called Bess Hawes, Alan Lomax's sister, and with her help arranged for Bessie Jones and the Sea Island Singers to attend the festival. The New Lost City Ramblers were a group that tried to recreate early commercial country music and I booked them. Mike Seeger, one of the Ramblers, rediscovered Dock Boggs, a coal miner, old-time singer, song writer and banjo player, and I invited him to perform. Blues men Brownie McGhee and Sonny Terry were invited. Ballad singers Jean Richie and Frank Warner were booked, and Bill Monroe and The Blue Grass Boys agreed to attend.

The festival performers also included Pete Seeger, who arrived with the then unknown Judy Collins. She was pretty and talented, and the audience loved her. I also booked song writer John Jacob Niles. Bill Monroe and his Blue Grass Boys arrived with Ralph Rinzler, who was their manager and who coined the phrase "The Father of Blue Grass Music' to describe Monroe.

American Folk Festival – brochure

Alan Lomax was concert Master of Ceremonies, adding informed commentary, directing most of the performances and frequently dictating what the artists played.

The American Folk Festival drew good audiences. Unlike Lunsford's festivals, there were no commercial sponsors and I relied on box office income to cover all costs.

The festival ended with a small loss, paid off in subsequent months.

I was not able to continue past the first year, but judging from public reaction the American Folk Festival was an artistic success. It provided visibility and recognition for the traditional artists involved, it contributed to a new, broader understanding of our cultural history, and it reached a new, more diverse audience

These memories were still vivid, and now, as the Smithsonian's impresario looking to bring life to the museums, I believed a folk festival would meet my objectives.

I also thought a festival could address elements of American cultural life missing from existing programs and exhibitions. And I hoped a festival might move the institution from a keeper and researcher of rare objects and curiosities to a forum for examining the plurality and diversity in American life.

FOUR

The Festival Idea

In the early weeks of 1967 I wrote Secretary Ripley proposing a Smithsonian folk festival. I emphasized that the Institution had a long history with the materials of folk culture. I also made the case that a festival would serve people at risk of cultural or social exclusion. In case Ripley needed more convincing, I added that the Institution's political and public relations would benefit.

I described the festival program I had in mind and requested a modest budget of $8900 covering artist fees and transportation. Ripley approved the festival idea, but allowed only $4,900 to cover fees and transportation.

His response did not express any particular enthusiasm for the festival idea, and I had serious doubts that a program meriting the name 'festival' could be accomplished for $4,900.

Perhaps I should have scuttled the whole idea, but by now I believed the festival would establish a signature program for the new Division of Performing Arts, a program quite different from the projects I had inherited. I thought back to

Ripley's eloquent public statements about enlivening the museums. Was that just a quotable posture? I really didn't know the man.

Nevertheless, I strongly believed a festival would bring life and new meaning to the collections and humanize the Smithsonian. Yet proceeding with a crippled budget was risky and failure would likely have an impact on any other opportunities.

It was hard to make a personal appeal to Ripley who was away from Washington. Instead I turned to Under Secretary Jim Bradley for help and advice. He promised unspecified help and suggested I try to raise private funds.

I had done all the programming for the Asheville festival, with suggestions from Alan Lomax and others. It was enjoyable work, but time consuming. Now I knew I needed help and I assigned Marian Hope, a new staff member and a savvy lady, to survey the folk scene. Calls to the Newport Folk Festival, the Pennsylvania Folk Festival and other sources yielded the name of Ralph Rinzler. I remembered Ralph in Asheville, as Bill Monroe's manager, and he was now doing field research for the Newport Festival. He was not an academic folklorist-he graduated from Swarthmore College with a major in French-but he had done good work for Newport.

Ralph's lack of academic folk culture credits didn't concern me. I admired several record albums of traditional music that he produced for Folkways Records. I thought his ability to work successfully with Bill Monroe and other performers showed qualities that were important. He had performed with The Greenbrier Boys, a folk revival group, and his association with Newport was very important. In addition, Alan Lomax added his strong endorsement.

Jim Bradley provided enough money for a short-term consulting contract, and I hired Ralph. His responsibility was to "help identify traditional folk musicians for Smithsonian performances". He came to Washington and we talked about my ideas for a Smithsonian festival. Soon he began to spend two or three days per week in our office.

At the American Folk Festival, as it was in Newport, the central program focus was an evening concert. For a Smithsonian festival I wanted to keep the evening performances, but emphasize smaller, more informal settings–places where listeners were in close proximity to the artists. I wanted an environment that encouraged communication between artists and audience, one where listeners might, for a few moments, enter the artist's world.

Ralph and I worked together, planning a balanced festival program. We worked well together, and I believed a genuine friendship was established. It was understood that I would somehow raise the necessary funds.

In one of our consultations, Ralph showed me an essay by a young folklorist named Henry Glassie. He wrote about 'folklife,' detailing how Scandinavian museums developed a concept that broadened presentations of folk culture to include the skills, work processes, celebrations, food ways–the entire life-style of a community. The idea was intriguing to me and we looked for ways to include 'folklife' in the festival program. We began to call the invited artists 'participants.' The name *Smithsonian Festival of American Folklife* was chosen and the July 4th weekend was the date.

I found the money we needed in a wide variety of sources. Some festival participants came from Appalachia and the Carolina's, Virginia and Georgia arts establishments contributed stipends and travel expenses. Greyhound Bus Lines provided free transportation for West Virginia fiddlers and a metal worker from Pennsylvania. Alaska Airlines paid for the participation of King Island Eskimo musicians and dancers. A Louisiana fish processing company sponsored a Cajun string band and private donors underwrote the costs of a panpipe player and drummer from Memphis, Tennessee. Ralph suggested a tale-teller from Lock No.4, Pennsylvania and a neighbor drove the man to Washington and paid his motel expenses. The New Mexico State Police helped locate a recommended stone carver and took up a collection to pay for his transportation. Ralph got a contribution of corn shucks to supply a doll maker. To provide wool for spinning and weaving demonstrations, weaver Norman Kennedy appealed to a friend with a supply of fleece from spring shearing. Small donors paid for Chinese, Irish and Russian musicians and dancers. North Carolina clog dancers raised money from local sponsors. Gospel singers from Alabama were sponsored by their church, a Puerto Rican band and a New Orleans jazz band were sponsored by tourism promoters. I found other sponsors for Blues singers, Native American singers, a blacksmith and a silversmith.

I made the majority of funding appeals, but Ralph was helpful in getting money for a Georgia potter and additional Cajun performers. His ability to do more was limited, in part, because he was a consultant, not a Smithsonian official.

And so it went, with every spare moment on the telephone in pursuit of financial help. The Smithsonian's $4900 was used to pay for logistics and the few participants who received no local support.

Each participant was paid a $100 honorarium. I was embarrassed to offer that meager amount but no one complained. All seemed honored to be invited to the national museum to sing or play or demonstrate their crafts.

About 70% of our fund-raising appeals were turned down, so a 30% success rate was good when compared to similar cases.

I contacted several Museum of History and Technology curators and asked for crafter recommendations but received no replies. The museum staff seemed not to know what to make of the Division of Performing Arts or the Festival of American Folklife. Several of the Museum of Natural History staff, particularly the anthropology curators, expressed some interest and were generally supportive, as was the Museum of American Art staff.

The Washington Star newspaper gave us some space, but there was no reporter on their staff who knew enough about folk culture to write knowledgeably. New York City's *Village Voice* paper was interested–not surprisingly–given the crowds of folkniks that populated Washington Square Park. The Washington Folklore Society members provided some hospitality and enthusiastic support.

Despite a few encouraging signs, I had no idea how the general public would receive the Festival.

FIVE

The Festival of American Folklife

The first *Smithsonian Festival of American Folklife* took place on the National Mall in Washington, D. C. from July 1 through July 4, 1967. In press releases, The National Park Service was credited as co-sponsor and provided security and crowd control.

In the final wrap-up the Park Service estimated Festival attendance at 380,000 people, making it the largest single audience for any event in the Smithsonian's history.

We had placed the Festival on the Mall, near the Museum of History and Technology, and across from the original Smithsonian building. The National Mall, the greensward referred to as the 'people's park' added symbolic significance. Festival participants were sheltered by a series of colorful tents laid out beneath the trees that shaded the expanse. The shade was provided by the Mall's beautiful, indigenous American elm trees. Distinguished by their grand canopies, these beautiful trees grow to a height of more than one hundred feet.

A remarkable crowd showed up for the Festival. Many came early and stayed all day and the Park Police noted that people were respectful and enthusiastic listeners.

The ethnic and social diversity of the participants was mirrored by the visitors. There were couples and individuals, stay-at-home moms and working people, a surprising number of 'suits,' large groups of young people-high school and college aged. I saw a lot of senior citizens. Someone told me that many were New Deal veterans, referencing a period when idealistic types came to Washington to work for the Roosevelt administration. And many, many families.

In the spring I had worried about our press coverage. At the time the local newspapers were genre-oriented in their cultural coverage. Critics specialized in writing about music, about theater, occasionally about dance – but little was written about folk culture. The Festival did have a champion in the person of *Washington Star* reporter Herman Schaden. From the outset, Schaden understood the festival idea and he wrote informative and entertaining stories which caught the attention of the *Washington Post*, the *New York Times* and other publications. Several major radio stations carried lengthy interviews and feature stories. The Smithsonian's Office of Public Affairs reported a record amount of press in attendance and some months later the Post introduced its new Style section, with broader reporting of cultural events.

After the Festival, Ripley wrote several people who had provided personal references for my appointment. One such

44

was North Carolina Senator Everett Jordan, a long-time family friend. Ripley wrote

Dear Senator Jordan,   July 13, 1967

    The great success of our recent folk festival on the Mall prompts me to tell you how pleased we have been with Jim Morris. Working with extremely limited resources, and in the face of a series of breathless deadlines, Jim performed like a true professional. He designed the festival, assembled the participants from all over the country and saw to it that everything went off with great éclat and high spirits. I think the folk festival will become an annual event in Washington by popular demand. We are grateful to you for telling us about Jim.

                    Sincerely,
                    S. Dillon Ripley

    A similar letter was sent to Senator Pell, with copies to Charles Blitzer, director of the Smithsonian's Office of Educational Programs.

    Ripley did not attend this first Festival, but Under Secretary Jim Bradley attended in his place. Bradley also dispatched a contingent of museum carpenters, technicians and electricians, plus a labor crew that operated sound systems and erected tents and stages. The Smithsonian travel office worked overtime to bring participants to the Mall and to see them safely home.

The small Division of Performing Arts staff showed great initiative. I worked with the set-up crew.

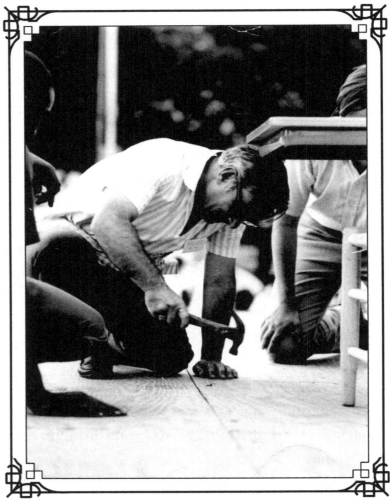

"...everybody pitches in."

Marian Hope published a handbook that provided participant orientation. Kesa Sakai turned her artist eye to the site plan and Beth Fine and Jeanette Gladstone maintained the steady flow of memos, requisitions, and permits while Meredith Johnson and Leslie Schaberg acted as un-official hosts, welcoming everyone, and Tim Jecko was a supportive deputy.

Ralph Rinzler continued as our consultant during the Festival. It helped that he had a personal relationship with some of the participants, particularly Doc Watson and Dewey Balfa. We collaborated on a running order of musical selections. Ralph was an occasional stage interlocutor and MC, and assisted the crafts people in setting up and demonstrating.

Ralph made another important contribution, suggesting a conference of scholars to see the Festival and comment on the Smithsonian's future role in folk-culture study and presentation. No money remained in Ripley's original allowance, but I argued for additional conference funds. Ripley liked the association with scholars and agreed to the money. I invited Alan Lomax, Archie Green, Moses Asch, Roger Abrahams, Don Yoder, Austin Fife, D. K. Wilgus and Richard Dorson, plus Smithsonian museum staff.

We wanted to sell crafts to Festival visitors but the museum shops were reluctant to leave the museum and move onto the Mall. Instead, we hired Roger Paige, a young college student, rented a U-Haul truck and sent him on a buying trip to several southern and Appalachian crafters. The crafts sold well and opened the way for continued craft sales in the museum shops.

My first nine months as a Smithsonian official had been remarkable. In addition to the Senatorial letters, I got a personal note from Ripley expressing his gratitude that I had brought life to the museums. I had solved the carousel problem, dealt with the Son et Lumier production and brought new energy and focus to Peggy Wood's plan for an *American College Theater Festival.*

Would the Folklife Festival have lasting significance? Time would tell, but I didn't have to wait to experience a personal feeling of joy as I watched the Festival in operation. Despite the large crowds, there had been no behavior problems. People were unfailingly polite and courteous, and participants were treated with warmth and respect. And the Mall was alive! When I looked at the expressions on the faces of those who attended, I felt we had tapped into some strong sense of community and goodwill that everyone shared.

I also felt a great personal sense of fulfillment at what we had created. For more than twenty years I had been a performer. As a singer, actor, director or conductor, I had never been far from the stage. And previously, when I had thought that I might give up performing, events drew me back. Now I was content to present others, happy to provide a setting where American artists and American culture could be seen and understood. It was a new and rewarding feeling.

There was one sour note. Several weeks after the Festival I was asked to meet with the curatorial staff of the Museum of History and Technology. About 50 people attended. The meeting began with a sharp critique about the Festival program, about the selection of musicians and crafts people and complaints that curators with expertise in material culture subjects had not been consulted. I was surprised, and hurt by the attacks, because I had requested advice and suggestions from the museum staff and had received no response. Their lack of response told me that I had more work to do to involve the curatorial community. It also told me something about Ripley's frustrated attempts to enliven the museums. And given the public's reception of the Festival, it showed a great deal about the staff's reluctance to get on board a moving train. At last, Silvio Bedini, assistant director of the museum, interceded, the meeting ended and I went my way. Later, a few of those present apologized.

SIX

Wooden Actors, Music Machines and Outreach

The success of the Folklife Festival was very gratifying, but there was fruit to be picked in other orchards. Ripley was interested in outreach–in extending the Smithsonian's resources and new enlivening experiences-beyond the Washington area. I was also interested in bringing life to neglected spaces and to other, under-served audiences, including children. I thought these goals were compatible.

Many museum exhibitions were stuffy. Labels meant to explain the exhibitions were written for adults and posted too high for young readers to see. To be successful at enlivening the museums and the Mall, we needed to speak the language of the young. I wanted young visitors to have fun during their Smithsonian visit.

In 1967 we erected a tent near the Castle and invited children to discover the historic enchantment of the theater. We presented two of the world's great puppet and marionette theater groups.

First was the *Theater Spejbl and Hurvinek,* the world's first state-sponsored, professional marionette theater, presented with financial help from the Czech embassy. They charmed children with adaptations of classic European folk tales and music. The marionettes came with a large company of live actors to pull their strings. Language was not a barrier, and none of their creativity was wasted on the young audiences.

Following S&H, as they became known, we presented *The Wooden Actors of Jacques Chenier,* from Paris. Chenier worked alone, and silently–save a simple musical tract. In a memorable scene, Chenier's character, Bip, entered the small stage and found a swing. After several tries, he discovered the swing moved to and fro. Then, seating himself on the swing, he made it move! Turning his wooden head toward the audience, with an air of profound satisfaction, he leaned back and enjoyed his wonderful discovery.

The children watched with rapt attention. I could not resist a whispered question to Chenier. "What do you call this piece?" I asked. "Happiness," was his answer. Oh, the power of imagination.

Exhibit designer Ben Lawless was equally enchanted. With his help an empty gallery in the museum was converted to *The Discovery Theater* .

We used theater performances to attract young audiences, but also to signal children that a museum was a place to play, a place for lively, enjoyable learning. The Discovery Theater continues today, presenting special, educational entertainments that welcome children to the museums and galleries.

In August we placed a stage out-of-doors, on the porch of the History and Technology Museum, the site of a gleaming, rotating metal sculpture designed by world-famous artist Alexander Calder. At dark the kinetic sculpture cast changing shadow forms on the porch floor and museum walls. In front of Calder's sculpture, we presented a performance by the Erich Hawkins Dance Theater, the dancers moving in counter-point against the shadows - a memorable sight! It was one of Washington's earliest exposures to American modern dance.

In December we converted the museum's empty Iron and Steel Hall into a forest of evergreen trees. I adapted a medieval mummers play, adding music and movement. We borrowed a large, papier-mache' dragon from sculptor Peter Schumann's Bread and Puppet Theater. Twice a day, for two weeks, an actor, portraying a comic Saint George, subdued the fearsome fire-breathing dragon and saved the world, to the accompaniment of songs and dancing. There was a full audience for every performance, and several curators asked that the production become an annual event. The curators of the Iron and Steel Hall were loathe to agree to any future use of their space and the possibility died.

The 19th century Arts and Industries building, also known as the National Museum, was the second oldest Smithsonian building. Originally erected to house the collections of the 1876 Centennial Exposition, the building had become the least visited Smithsonian museum. It also has the most fanciful architecture on the Mall, with a high roof and open galleries. In an effort to enliven the space, an orchestrion, an automated music machine, was installed.

Built in Germany in the 19th century and dubbed *The Mighty Music Machine*, it sounded like a combined brass band, piano, drum and bugle ensemble plus numerous sound effects. It serenaded audiences on the hour. Then we presented a concert of the songs of American composer Charles Ives, featuring the Gregg Smith Singers, a premier vocal ensemble. With singers dispersed throughout the building, their voices reverberating in antiphonal effect, the concert drew high praise from the audience and critics.

At the Museum of Natural History's Baird Auditorium, we presented a staged reading of *The Victory of Socrates*. Veteran motion picture star and character actor Walter Abel contributed his time and experience, aided by a cast of local actors. Abel was very able, injecting as much drama as possible to a script that was too wordy. The reading was an attempt to recapture a famous dialogue, but the moment resisted enlivenment.

To introduce audiences to Asian theater, we then presented performances of Japan's classical Kyogen Theater. The Baird was an ideal setting for a theater genre that relied on gesture, posture and subtle inflection. The company of actors and technicians were brilliantly trained and were funded in part by the Asian Society, in part by the Japanese embassy. We joined forces with other foreign embassies to present renowned touring chamber music ensembles from Eastern Europe.

I had proposed concerts of jazz but there was no funding. Instead, we partnered with The Left Bank Jazz Society to present a series of concerts by major jazz artists.

While arranging these performances, I continued to study Smithsonian exhibitions and resources. An informal survey led to a surprising and troubling discovery. In the Museum of History and Technology, no exhibit, no object, no label or photo panel recognized the presence of black Americans. While the Museum of Natural History had ethnographic exhibitions of African tribal life, the museum devoted to American history did not seem to recognize the history and culture of Afro-Americans — nor their role in American life and society.

By now, I knew most of the executives, the senior staff, administrators, museum directors, bureau chiefs, and curators. I did not think they were racists. They were experts in their fields, aware of their academic and social class, comfortable and unchallenged in their status. For the most part they were thoughtful, caring people. But they were all white. What then to make of the cultural and social exclusion evinced in the exhibitions? And my concerns were not limited to black Americans but extended to Latino and other minorities. Could the Performing Arts programs we were developing redress some of the imbalance? I believed they could.

Then, in 1968, the Division of Performing Arts, the Office of Education, the Smithsonian Associates, the Smithsonian Press and Smithsonian Magazine (then in its planning stage) were grouped together under a new Assistant Secretary for Public Service, to be led by William Warner. He was known to friends and colleagues as "Willie." He was a veteran of the Peace Corps and an altogether decent man. That same year

Willie's book, *Beautiful Swimmers*, about the Chesapeake Bay, won the Pulitzer Prize for Literature.

The Folklife Festival continued to draw praise, and moved closer to becoming an established event. With increased funds, I requested an additional staff position in order to hire Ralph Rinzler as a full-time employee. I intended to name him Festival Director, and myself Festival Producer. Some members of the Secretariat questioned Ralph's lack of appropriate academic credentials. No one questioned my credentials, which were entirely professional and not academic. But I wasn't interested in the academic argument–I was interested in hiring someone with proven field research experience that would lead to the identification of Festival participants. With Willie's help I managed to overcome the objections.

Word of the Festival's success spread rapidly. There were new outreach opportunities when agencies in Virginia and North Carolina asked for advice with programs. I spent several days advising the City of New Orleans on plans for a jazz and heritage festival, and Governor Winthrop Rockefeller of Arkansas contacted Ripley, asking him to send 'Smithsonian experts' to Arkansas to attend an arts meeting. Ripley agreed and chose me as 'an expert,' along with Richard Cowan, director of the Museum of Natural History.

Cowan and I were met by Rockefeller's plane in Little Rock and flown to Winrock Farm, his elaborate ranch and cattle farm atop Petit Jean Mountain overlooking the Arkansas River. Winthrop was a 3rd generation member of the wealthy Rockefeller family. The announced purpose of our visit was to help plan for an Arkansas cultural center.

At Winrock, we were taken to luxurious guest quarters adjacent to the main house. I remember the scene-the late edition of national newspapers in each room, the servants in attendance, the prepared snacks in the refrigerator, the marbled bath, the scented soap (the soap was replaced daily), the terry robes, the huge vase filled with flowers (the flowers were changed daily), the gardens and manicured landscaping, the carpeted, air conditioned barns that housed prized cattle. I thought being rich must be very pleasant. A newspaper headline reported that the assembly had set the Arkansas governor's salary at $10,000 per year.

There were ten or more guests for dinner, all men. The food was excellent–small game hens with wild rice and several salads and pastries. Excellent wine.

Governor Rockefeller was an uncomfortable, awkward host and conversation did not happen easily. Finally, at brandy and cigars, he asked if there were questions about Winrock, our accommodations, the state or other subjects. There was a heavy silence. I felt his discomfort and was sorry for him. Finally I said, "Governor. Today's press reports your yearly salary at $10,000?" "Yes?" he replied. "How do you manage to live like this on $10,000 per year?" I asked.

He laughed. Really laughed! A good, long, belly laugh. The others followed suit. It was the first time I had heard so much as chuckle since my arrival.

I had been rash and was afraid my question would seem audacious and make everyone uncomfortable. On the contrary, it seemed to break the ice. Everyone smiled and conversation was eased. And Governor Rockefeller? He treated me like an adopted son, sitting next to me at meetings and lunch.

We spent two days at Winrock. I don't think we contributed many ideas to the cultural center discussions, but in the fall I returned, with Ralph, to Mountain View, Arkansas. This time we were invited by Jimmy Driftwood to see his work with a small, regional organization.

Jimmy was a model of charm, ingenuity, entrepreneurship, and musical talent. In 1968 he was a nationally known folk singer, song writer, instrumentalist and teacher.

Born and raised on a small Arkansas farm, he was living and farming in Timbo, Arkansas when we visited.

Jimmy's story reflected the model. He passed the state teacher's examination at age 16 and started teaching in rural schools at 17. Recognizing that his students were struggling with the complexities of history, his solution was to write songs about historic events. He accompanied himself on a fiddle and a guitar his father made from a piece of rail fence. He was a gifted story teller, and his songs became popular with his students. In 1959, one of those songs, *The Battle of New Orleans,* recorded by Johnny Horton, topped the sales charts for 10 weeks and received numerous Grammy nominations. Jimmy became a star of The Grand Ole Opry, and in his lifetime wrote some 6,000 songs, including the popular *Tennessee Stud.*

Not content with stardom, Jimmy returned to his Timbo farm, where he helped organize The Rackensack Folklore Society and raised money for a regional water system. When we met he was pursuing a Federal grant to build the Ozark Folk Center State Park.

Jimmy Driftwood was his stage name. His given name was James Morris, a coincidence that amused both Jimmy and me. Our amusement was amplified by the fact that we both had sons of a similar age—and both sons were also named James Morris. I told Jimmy, "if we keep this up we could create some real confusion."

Returning to Washington, we began to work on the second Folklife Festival. We thought an interesting idea would be to achieve an outreach partnership with a regional American theme. I had seen a press release about *HemisFair '68*, the first international exposition held in the southwestern United States. San Antonio, Texas, was the host city. The article described the Texas Pavilion – *The Institute of Texan Cultures* – as a center for multi-cultural education.

Ralph went to San Antonio to see what the Institute of Texan Cultures (ITC) was about.

He reported that it was an exhibition of artifacts reflecting the settlement of the state, including the German, French, Czech, Polish, Afro-American, Chicano and Anglo communities. We approached the ITC exhibition managers about a Texas theme at the Folklife Festival, focusing on living Texas folklife. There was interest. We created a budget, and in true Texas style, the money was raised with a phone call. The ITC managers began work with us on our first regional theme.

With more funds from the Smithsonian, a good sponsor for the Texas theme plus better lead time, we were able to move closer to the 'folklife' concept. Ralph directed the field research effort, making use of previous work by the University of Texas and other folk culture programs. He negotiated a large food-ways component that involved a crew to cook barbecue, corn on the cob and a variety of ethnic foods.

I thought it was a very good festival program, with interesting crafts people, cooks, cowboy singers, blues shouters and ballad singers, and Mexican-American tejano and conjunto bands from Texas.

The Texas participants' whooping, the electrifying yodel of the Oinkari Basque Dancers from Idaho and the shouts of powerful gospel singers made it a rich cultural smorgasbord.

Because of his Texas roots, Alan Lomax was invited to emcee the evening concert. Ralph was concerned about Alan's tendency to dictate program choices, but we developed a comfortable working relationship. Alan was very supportive of the Festival, but I was not happy when he called Ripley and arranged a one-on-one meeting without consulting me or Ralph. It was typical of Alan, who had a strong and disturbing need to seize control of any situation. After the meeting, Alan said he told Ripley that the team of Morris and Rinzler, producer and field researcher, was ideal and should be supported.

Following Lomax's stage appearance Ripley received hostile letters from several members of Congress. The letters, passed on to me to reply, alleged Lomax was involved with communist-front organizations – charges that had been made before. We had taped Lomax' stage remarks, which spoke about "the rivers of song that flowed from the folk," and "the art that the American people had created from their own experiences."

I made copies of the remarks and sent them to the Congressmen and we heard no more complaints.

SEVEN

Folklife at the XIX Olympiad

In 1968 the eyes of many in the world were focused on the Summer Games of the XIX Olympiad to be held in Mexico City. It was the first Olympic Games to be hosted by a third world country. Along with the athletic competition is the image competition. The Mexican organizers chose to boost their image by adding cultural events to the sweat and strive endeavors.

Participating nations were asked to send exhibitions or performances that exemplified their ethos, an idea originated by the great Mexican National Museum of Anthropology. Museum officials visited several international cities, seeking non-commercial programs that fit their vision. In Washington they visited the Smithsonian and saw the Folklife Festival. They immediately contacted the U. S. Department of State, requesting that American Olympic participation be produced by the Smithsonian's Division of Performing Arts.

The Mexican request surprised the State Department and shocked the Smithsonian management. Requests of this nature were usually made through diplomatic channels, leaving the selection of producers to the discretion of State's Assistant Secretary for Cultural Affairs. The Smithsonian was shocked because the Division of Performing Arts original mission was to enliven the museums and the Mall. Ripley had already expanded that mission, adding outreach to our tasks. Now the Mexican request wanted us to function as a producer of an international cultural event..

I thought we should accept the assignment. Producing an Olympic cultural event would be major outreach and add to our visibility and fund-raising posture. And income from a State Department contract would support the next Festival.

After several State Department/Smithsonian meetings the matter was resolved: The Division of Performing Arts of the Smithsonian Institution would produce for the U. S. Department of State a two-week long celebration of American folk culture. The celebration would be funded entirely by the Department of State and what we produced would be the official American participation in the Olympic Cultural Program.

As we began work I learned that the State Department envisioned an 'American folk music and dance *Company*.' Their model was Mexico's Ballet Folklorico, Russia's Moiseyev Dance Company or the Don Cossacks Choir.

The Mexican/Russian folk company model involved studio trained, choreographed performers. The Cossack's Choir used trained singers performing choral arrangements of folk songs. All these folk companies performed in colorfully costumes designed by professional designers, staged by professional directors and supported by theatrical lighting. The Olympic officials wanted the authentic, unselfconscious performers seen at the Folklife Festival.

Ralph and I worked together to select an Olympic program. We chose ballad singer Jean Ritchie, bluegrass banjo player Don Stover, fiddler Tex Logan, guitarist Doc Watson and panpipe player and drummer Ed and Lonnie Young. We also chose blues man Bukka White, an Afro-American tap-dance duo, the Georgia Sea Island Singers and the Blue Ridge Mountain Cloggers. Then we decided to include a small jazz ensemble and four members of the Harlem-based Afro-American Dancers. Altogether they were strong representatives of our cultural heritage.

Developing a presentational concept was an uncomfortable responsibility. There were budgetary limits and many good artists could not be included. Of those selected, Anglo-Afro artists predominated, outnumbering artists from other ethnic groups. We had no unifying visual concept or production values (costumes, props, set pieces, projections etc). Ralph was strongly opposed to the use of theatrical techniques. I argued that we were, after all, performing in theaters.

Our different points of view – theatrical style versus authenticity - led to interpersonal tensions that, in time, came to define my relationship with Ralph. In many ways I shared Ralph's preferences. I liked hearing folk performers in their natural settings, singing and playing as they might in their parlor or on their porch, and my original festival presentational ideas reflected my preferences. And I did not like what happened when authentic folk performers were situated on a large stage in a theatrical environment. Too often I had seen and heard discontent and self-consciousness replace a natural, relaxed attitude. In those circumstances I believed we were not showing the care and respect authentic folk artists deserved. I also was aware that Lomax, Bert Lloyd and other champions of 'the folk' had not hesitated to use theatrical techniques.

Mexico City was colorful. Driving into the city from the airport, we passed a shifting landscape of vibrant color. To obscure the ubiquitous urban poverty, the Mexican government had distributed large amounts of colored paint. Adobe huts, frame houses, plywood shacks, outhouses, reed fences, tiny shops and small factory walls, even the occasional automobile - any available surface was covered in paint. Residents and owners were allowed any color selection-yellow or blue or green or orange or purple and from every direction surfaces returned the bright blaze of the Mexican sun.

There were also tensions. Before the Olympics there were protests by political factions opposed to the cost of the games. Forces of the Mexican military were called to quell the protest. Shots were fired and protesters were killed.

During the games, American sprinters Tommie Smith and John Carlos each won medals. At the medal presentation, Smith and Carlos raised their hands in acknowledgement and their hands were covered by black gloves – a black power salute.

Olympic and American officials were surprised, insulted and upset. Recriminations and apologies dominated the press coverage and the spirits of our small company of artists were dampened. Afro-American participants discussed a boycott, or leaving for home. I met with the group. There was venting and verbal tensions. Racial animosities were acknowledged and discussed, as was the news playing out on television. But cool heads prevailed and we were not forced to cancel any performances.

Our troupe played two performances each day at diverse venues, including Mexico City's elaborate 1934 opera house, the Palacio de Bellas Artes. We performed in outdoor amphitheaters, in two parks and in several small outdoor theaters. Everywhere, Mexican audiences were receptive, and there were some memorable and touching moments. Mexican dancers and musicians responded strongly to the Appalachian clog dance and Tex Logan's fiddling style. They had a difficult time copying the straight-backed, rigid attitude of the American dancers, and Logan's aggressive bowing style was hard to master, but they enjoyed trying. Latin guitarists attempted to copy Doc Watson's flat-picking skills. The jazz performances, the tap dancing duo and the Harlem Afro-American foursome regularly drew the most prolonged applause. After the first performances, the white artists accepted the inevitability with tight smiles.

In the end the State Department reported that our performances were a success. The press wrote complimentary things about the Smithsonian. The American ambassador hosted a marvelous party, there were smiles and kind words for everyone involved and all the artists enjoyed being tourists. I was skeptical, unsure that an American 'folk music and dance company' would ever be more than a curiosity. It felt like we were pushing a round peg into a square hole.

We returned to Washington and to planning a season of performances, plus the 1969 Folklife Festival. Then disaster struck.

Ralph, two field researchers and two friends were on their way to a Polish festival in Pennsylvania when their van was blindsided by a large truck. Three of the passengers were hospitalized with multiple injuries. Ralph's injuries were the most severe and he was lucky to be alive.

I was attending a conference in New York when word of the accident reached me. I immediately left for Washington and the George Washington University Hospital. Entering the hospital room I saw Ralph's leg suspended in traction. I could see that he was in considerable pain, with fractured leg and ribs, plus a concussion. The surgeon expressed concern that he would ever regain full use of his injured leg.

I sat by his bed for some time, hoping he would know how deeply concerned I was. We had developed an involved working relationship, sharing values and mutual goals. I also had come to think of him as a friend rather than an employee and I was determined to see that he got the best care available.

The 1969 Folklife Festival was to feature the State of Pennsylvania.

**Mary Ripley, Volunteers, Dillon Ripley and volunteers with
James Morris, Festival of American Folklife, 1969**

We had planned for Ralph to do much of the field
research, aided by folk culture students from the University
of Pennsylvania, but his accident changed things. We

discussed a cancellation – ruled it out, and looked for alternatives.

To cover Ralph's absence, I hired folklorist/writer Mack McCormick, while Ralph continued to work from his hospital bed. Ralph had a prior association with Mack that left both of them with trepidations that impeded a trusting work relationship, but they put the past aside. It was a very stressful time.

Mack did an excellent job, producing innovative program ideas and identifying potential sponsors. I was impressed with his fieldwork results, and inquired about his methods. "I often start with the phone book Yellow Pages," he said, "looking for unusual and innovative crafts people."

Despite the difficulties, a good Festival program came together. The incorporation of folklife elements expanded, with a Greek community celebration and a lumberjack competition. For a wool processing exhibition, sheep grazed on the Mall, occasionally herded by sheep dogs. The sheep were sheared and their wool washed to the sound of singing. Then the wool was carded and spun, the spun wool dyed, dried and woven into cloth. A tailor cut the cloth to garment measurements and a fascinated audience saw the entire process, from sheep to shawl.

In a first for Festival programming, we brought a Toby Show to the Mall. The Toby company came with their tent, decorated with humorous local advertising, their hand made props, their family band and their bumpkin costumes. On stage, Toby was always the hero and the central character in their decades-old farces, written by unknown authors and performed in a style handed down from generation to generation. There were two standing-room-only performances each day by this unique folk theater, the last of its kind in the United States.

Several weeks after Ralph's accident, I received word that my father had died. His death was sudden—a heart attack that came as he waited to lunch with friends. I left immediately for the family home in Greensboro, N. C.

My father's death unleashed a flood of powerful memories.

James Rouse Morris Sr. had shaped my life by his values, his compassion and his courage. He had been the treasurer of the Guilford County Democratic Party for thirty years, a passionate liberal, devoted supporter of Franklin Roosevelt, keen-eyed baseball umpire and loving parent.

He was the son of a Methodist minister who continued that ministry by teaching the largest Sunday school class in North Carolina. He survived the Great Depression by refusing to give in to despair. He survived a disastrous auto accident by refusing to accept disability. He survived heart disease with humor and unflinching courage. He loved me without any conditions or reservations, and I miss him very much.

EIGHT

The Theater on the Mall

When Secretary Ripley met with actress Peggy Wood, he pledged Smithsonian support for a National College Theater Festival. Of course he knew that the Smithsonian did not have a theater to house such an event, so he suggested the Smithsonian could provide a temporary tent theater. Ms. Wood was no dummy. She accepted Ripley's commitment and carried it with her when she approached other potential sponsors-and when she enlisted support from members of Congress. When she had firm commitments from Roger Stevens and the Kennedy Center, the National Educational Theater Association and various commercial groups, Ripley and the Smithsonian were obligated to sponsor the Festival.

The legislation creating the Kennedy Center makes the Center an independent bureau of the Smithsonian. Occasionally Ripley would send me, as his surrogate, to meetings of the Center's Board of Directors. I was present when Center Chairman Stevens reported a start-up grant of $5,000 to the College Theater Festival Committee. Stevens turned to me and asked if Ripley was prepared to make a similar commitment. I had to say that I did not know Mr. Ripley's plans.

Stevens replied "If Dillon wants to 'liven up' the Smithsonian by sponsoring activities like the Theater Festival he should put up some cash."

As Smithsonian Impresario I was responsible for meeting Ripley's commitment. I was also the only member of the staff who had any knowledge of theater operations. Liv Biddle's had said "there are not many people with your experience" – and I remembered some of those experiences.

After study at the Juilliard School of Music, I became an apprentice at the Fort Worth Civic Opera, where they mounted several major productions each season. My mentor and coach was Karl Kritz, the Opera's music director. Kritz was also a Metropolitan Opera conductor, and a product of the disciplined and exacting world of German opera. He insisted I learn all the roles in each production plus all the elements of theater mise-en-scene. He also had me learn about the history and protocols of theater production. It was a good experience.

After a season in Fort Worth, I moved on to paid employment at the State Fair Musicals in Dallas, where I worked in six productions in twelve weeks and learned about musical theater from Broadway's Lehman Engle[1].

_____

[1] Lehman Engle wrote *The American Musical; a Consideration*

In his legendary career, Lehman had conducted numerous Broadway productions, composed original music, produced recordings and won six Tony Awards. He also founded BMI's Lehman Engle Musical Theater Workshop, an important development program for composers, lyricists, and libretti writers. Lehman knew the stage, and taught the elements of effective musical theater production. I listened as he explained scenarios and musical composition, plot and character development; pacing, emphasis and focus; plus stage management and direction. Lehman said, "In the best musicals there is a seamless construction. Sequences of song, dance and dialogue are knit together in an unbroken unit. The stitches are not seen by the audience, the flow of action runs through the scenes without a break, our concentration unbroken. Our American musical theater does this better than any theater form in history."

After Dallas I returned to New York City, and study with Joe Moon and Ernestine Perrie. Joe had been music director for Alfred Lunt and Lynn Fontaine, and musical assistant to Irving Berlin and Cole Porter. At the time Joe was an important teacher and coach of aspiring Broadway actors and singers, and taught me a lot about the skills and traditions of performing in musicals, plus the enjoyment of colorful characters who give the theater its patina. Joe also took me to the country house of theater and motion picture star Tallulah Bankhead, where we wined and dined, swam nude in Ms. Bankhead's pool, and laughed at her oft-quoted remark, "If I had my life to live again, I'd make the same mistakes, only sooner!"

Theater studies with Ernestine Perrie taught me about the importance of resources, research and detailed preparation, the foundation of productive rehearsals. Some of her theater genius may have been inherited. She was born into a troupe of actors, Italian immigrants who toured the United States, performing a repertory of plays for Italian communities on the east and west coasts. In their 50s her parents, Silvio and Esther Minciotti, were cast in numerous films and television plays, and Esther Minciotti played a starring role in the 1956 Academy Award film, *Marty*. 'Ernie' was an inspiring teacher, a person of great humanity and a brilliant stage director. When at work on a play or musical, Ernie examined all available evidence and questioned all assumptions. She taught that "the theater, at its best, was about the search for understanding, the study of how and why people speak and react to one another, and about the truths and emotions found in that search."

I made my Broadway debut when Ernie cast me in the verse play, *In April, Once*, by William Alexander Percy. The cast was full of Broadway veterans: Bill Penn had appeared in *The Fifth Season*, Page Johnson in *Camino Real* and *Romeo and Juliet*, Don McHenry in *The Crucible* and the film version of *Fanny*. Two other actors, Charles Durning and Vincent Gardenia achieved star status in several films and stage productions. I was the novice, and was thrilled when the New York Times theater critic said I "gave a bright, spirited performance."

A short time later I was hired by the New York City Opera Company for their spring season. I sang occasional small parts and in the ensemble in productions of *La Boheme, Manon, The Marriage of Figaro, La Traviata, Der Rosenkavalier, The Love for Three Oranges, Andrea Chenier, Cavalleria Rusticana, I Pagliacci, Wozzeck, The Old Maid and the Thief*, and the first stage production of *Amahl and the Night Visitors*–twelve productions in a few months. The experience was an intense learning test and a thorough evaluation of stage production and management assumptions.

My life was full of humor. I was serious, but joyful, and enriched by the acquaintance of many talented people, including the gifted but rebellious tenor David Poleri. Appearing in *Carmen* at the Chicago Opera, David disagreed with and challenged the conductor's tempos–an unheard of behavior in the opera world. In the final scene, as a jealous Don Jose moves to stab Carmen, David–as Jose‾threw down his knife and shouted to the shocked conductor, "Here, finish it yourself." As written, the opera must end with Carmen's death, but Jose had left Carmen alone on the stage! Then the quick-witted Carmen picked up the knife and killed herself.

Newspaper headlines screamed, "Carmen commits suicide in Chicago." Everyone, everywhere, was sure that David would be fired for such a heinous act! But good tenors are hard to find, and David was a very good tenor, and several months later he was back on stage in London, starring at the Royal Opera House Covent Garden to rave reviews from the press.

Several years later I was saddened when David and his new bride died in a plane crash.

♪♪♪

I believe the sum of these early experiences was an introduction to critical pedagogy and consciousness, a state which encourages, in the words of author Ira Shor, "habits of thought that go beneath surface meaning, first impressions, myths, official pronouncements and clichés."

Now I tried to "go beneath surface meaning" and understand Ripley's interest in a college theater festival. I fervently hoped it might signal an interest in the history of the theater as a vital force in American life. Instead, I learned that the congressperson who determined the Smithsonian's budget had a brother who was past president of the American Educational Theater Association and a key supporter of the theater festival.

So we were committed festival sponsors—but without a theater. A tent theater on the Mall? No funds had been allocated. Available circus tents would not accommodate set designs common to college and university productions. Tents used for social gatherings would not support adequate lighting instruments. Tensile membrane structures of the type designed by German architect Frei Paul Otto for Montreal's Expo 67 were marvelous, but too large and complicated-and too expensive. A Buckminster Fuller geodesic dome required costly modification.

The solution came from our own office. Richard Lusher, a talented theater designer had recently joined our staff, and he proposed a steel beam, camel-saddle design sufficient to meet technical requirements and seat seven hundred people. Smithsonian engineers studied the model and praised its ingenuity. But how were we to pay for it?

78

I had noticed that several companies were interested in marketing their products to college and university students and I thought they might be a source of money. I wrote a proposal and sent it to several of these sources, asking for funds to cover the cost of materials and labor. My proposal was endorsed by the National Park Service, custodians of the Mall. In a remarkably short time, Pepsi Cola responded, pledging a majority of the needed funds. General Motors followed, completing our budget.

Fund-raising is usually a lengthy proposition and I was surprised by the quick response. I learned later that film actress Joan Crawford, a member of Pepsi's board and wife of Pepsico's president, may have facilitated the contribution.

Smithsonian Assistant Secretary William Warner and National Capital Parks Director Nash Castro and I had a celebratory lunch. A theater that would be a resource for Smithsonian programs and exhibitions and the Park Service would have another venue for public events. And a number of museum colleagues offered congratulations.

The Theater on the Mall was completed in April 1969, and we put it to immediate use.

The first performance was by the Alwin Nikolais Dance Theater. Nikolais had trained in dance with Hanya Holm, Martha Graham and Charles Weidman and he was a master of stage movement, scenic design, puppetry and musical composition.

Next we turned to work that characterized America's reaction to the Great Depression. The Federal Theater Project of the Works Progress Administration (WPA) provided work for unemployed actors and artists. The WPA–some said the letters stood for Whistle, Piss and Argue, put thousands to work and spawned lasting activity in theater, painting, sculpture, architecture and music.

An important Federal Theater project was the Living Newspapers, plays created by journalists and actors that addressed important social issues, including farm policy, syphilis testing, and re-settlement. *Triple-A Plowed Under* dramatized the plight of dust bowl farmers. *One Third of a Nation* dramatized President Roosevelt's speech that said "I see one third of a nation ill-housed, ill-clad and ill-nourished."

I chose to produce *One Third of a Nation* because the story had remained relevant. The original production was too long and used a large company of actors. I edited the script, and with some careful pruning reduced the cast to 12 local actors. I staged the performances and the result was a powerful, emotional piece of theater. Public response was enthusiastic and ticket sales offset the production costs.

Next was the American College Theater Festival. Performances were divided between the Theater on the Mall and Ford's Theater. Joan Crawford and various film and stage celebrities attended the opening performance and Pepsi hosted an elaborate reception.

The chosen plays and musicals came from Los Angeles City College, Hofstra University, Ohio University, Oklahoma University, Wayne State University, the North Carolina School for the Arts, Pennsylvania State University, the University of Arizona, the University of Nebraska, Hanover College, Georgetown University, the University of Texas at Austin, Hampton Institute, Lea College on Lake Chapeau,

Cerritos College, Dartmouth College, Howard University and Boston University.

In the view of the press and the participants the American College Theater Festival was a success, and, in addition to performances, the Smithsonian hosted a symposium entitled *The American Theater – A Cultural Process.* The proceedings were published by Samuel French Books.

The Theater on the Mall continued to operate with daytime productions for young audiences and evening performances aimed at a general attendance. We planned to produce three classic American musicals: Irving Berlin's *Annie Get Your Gun*, George and Ira Gershwin's *Of Thee I Sing,* and Frank Loesser's *Guys And Dolls,* The theater was also used for performances during the third Festival of American Folklife I thought we might show how the American musical reflected the national experience and became a cultural icon. And I thought the shows would demonstrate another way to enliven the Mall.

Rehearsals for *Annie Get Your Gun* began in June 1969. Costumes and orchestra parts were rented from a recent Broadway revival, sets and lighting by Richard Lusher. The *Washington Star* critic wrote, "Morris staged it brightly and brassily, as befits the tale of Annie Oakley. Thanks to Irving Berlin there was always a good song not more than minutes away. The opening night audience was uncommonly appreciative; there ought to be more like it." The *Washington Post* critic wrote, "Even its first night, 23 years ago, could hardly have had a more enthusiastic reception." The *Washington Daily News* reported, "...the packed house loved every minute...the direction of James Morris left little room for improvement."

Annie Get Your Gun was the high point in the life of The Theater on the Mall. As the summer went on, it rained, and when it rained, the roof became a drum head and every drop a drum beat. At times the summer heat made the theater uncomfortable. There was praise for our efforts to turn the Mall from an empty urban space to a vibrant scene, with people strolling underneath the elms and enjoying the awesome views. There were attempts to find another location for the theater, but there were no funds and no adequate space was available. In the end, the theater was dismantled and sold.

1969 was also a year of personal tragedy. Our second child, Katherine, died after an unsuccessful operation for cystic fibrosis, and my wife fell into a deep and lasting depression. During the child's hospitalization, I had spent many hours in the waiting room, while Jimmy Morris stayed with Ralph Rinzler at his Capitol Hill home.

I was deeply saddened by Katherine's death. The personal burdens were almost unbearable and I took refuge in work.

While developing programs to enliven the museums and the Mall, I had struggled with ideas and theories about the nature of culture. When I lived and worked in Germany, I attended a series of lectures at Goethe University. The lecturer sorted genres into categories of high, popular and folk culture, a stratification well known to American social theorists. The categorical boundaries were arbitrary and I did not feel they fit the multi-cultural patterns of American culture. Nevertheless I thought categories might serve as an organizing principle for Smithsonian performances and special events.

I continued to spend much of my time raising funds. The Folklife Festival appeared to be established, yet the Smithsonian's appropriation left a large gap in our spending plans.

Then I attended a meeting of other impresarios, sponsored by the National Endowment for the Arts, and a plan evolved. I should 'institutionalize' the Festival – creating a distinct entity with its own budgetary line item. The new entity could be called the American Folklife Center. Apart from the Smithsonian's regular budget, it would be easily identified when Congress was making appropriations.

Jim Hightower, a legislative aid to Senator Ralph Yarborough and a long-time supporter of the Festival, took up the cause. Jim wrote a bill, S1591. It was sponsored by Senator Yarborough, and introduced, calling for the creation of a Folklife Center. There were hearings at various locations across the country. I had a busy production schedule to meet, but Ralph's time was more flexible and he worked to round up folklorists, writers and notable performers that testified in favor of the Center. There was also considerable public support for the idea, and the bill passed. The Folklife Center was established and the path to a direct appropriation was clear-but that path did not lead to the Folklife Festival or to the Smithsonian's Division of Performing Arts.

The Smithsonian, for reasons that were never clear to me, declined to give the Center a home. Instead, the Center was placed in the Library of Congress.

I was angry and perplexed. The Festival had been a substantial success for the Smithsonian. It was a major step toward enlivening the museums. It had garnered broad support for the Institution from members of Congress, the press and the public. Most of the cost of the event had been raised from private sources. It had led the Smithsonian toward a re-definition of cultural history. It had helped to change public perception of the Institution from an elitist, racially insensitive organization to an open, egalitarian educational establishment.

In refusing to accept the Folklife Center I thought I heard other messages. Perhaps the Division of Performing Arts had been established as an end run around the recalcitrance of museum directors and curators. Maybe I was supposed to push the museums into re-thinking their operating style. Perhaps we were just a change agent, created to address goals that the museums could not, or would not, adopt. And perhaps, when the initial goals had been met, we would be expendable. If there was truth here, it had never been discussed with me, and had never surfaced in policy discussions. It was a sobering thought. I didn't like it.

NINE

Popular Culture

By 1970 some of our performing arts initiatives had taken root. The Folklife Festival, the children's programs, the diverse musical activities were established and popular with the public and Congress, Festival participants came from every region and all were constituents of a member of Congress. Secretary Ripley was cited as the man who brought 'the common folk' to the Mall, and the association modified his patrician image.

I pondered the advantage of this popularity. As a next step in enlivening the Smithsonian, I wanted to begin the study and presentation of American popular culture.

I confess to influences from artists like Duke Ellington. When asked about his thoughts on jazz music and popular culture, the Duke responded with "It's difficult to decide where jazz starts and stops, where Tin Pan Alley begins and jazz ends, and where the borderline lies between classical music and jazz, I feel there is no borderline."

At the time, serious consideration of popular culture was relatively new to the academic world. It was certainly a new area for the Smithsonian, as the presentation of folk culture had been. Popular culture genres–literature, music, theater, film, recordings, television, mass media et al–were powerful engines of economic power. They were also vigorous cultural expressions. While the musical products of folk culture could be nostalgic, gentle, romantic and attitudinal, the products of popular culture were changeable, volatile, controversial, often vulgar, and on occasion political.

Years earlier I was part of that culture.

I was newly married and living in a dark, studio apartment on West 26nd Street in Manhattan. I was intensely involved in vocal and acting studies and making barely enough money to pay the rent and buy food.

Joe Moon, that marvelous vocal coach, was teaching me the skills needed to get television and recording jobs. He was also teaching me about the entertainment world, about it's operational particularities and some of it's values. I was very inexperienced, but making progress. Then, on a late summer morning, Joe called. "Clean up, put on some casual clothes and catch the subway to Columbus Circle," he said. "Go to the fourth floor of the Circle Building. There's a rehearsal room where you'll find Gordon Jenkins. He's A & R for Decca Records and he's casting singers for a new television variety show. Tell him I sent you."

I knew Jenkins' name, and knew he was Artists and Repertory chief at Decca Records. He was one of the most successful producers and arrangers in popular music. His recording of *Good Night, Irene*, with the Weavers, had been number one on the pop song charts for weeks.

Jenkins was a nice man. Unlike producers who treat auditioning singers like a lower form of life, Gordon was friendly and easy going. He asked me to sing, then told me to report for rehearsals in three weeks.

I had been hired for a television show, *The U. S. Royal Showcase*, a weekly network variety show broadcast by NBC-TV on Sunday evening. The host and director was George Abbott. Gordon Jenkins was the musical director and arranger.

I called to thank Joe, and he told me, "Pay attention to everything that happens, Watch what each guest star does, how they work, how they invent and create their moments. And pay particular attention to George Abbott, no one has a better understanding of the art in American theater."

He was always called "Mr. Abbott," his first name being strictly reserved for a few close friends. He began working in the theater in 1913, and by 1952, when he directed the *Showcase*, he had been involved in 86 Broadway productions. At various times he was an actor, a playwright, a producer, and a 'play doctor,' but he was best known as a director, and he had very firm ideas about directing. If you worked for Mr. Abbott you arrived at rehearsal on time and knew your part. You did not waste time on social conversation. You did not talk during rehearsal. If you had questions about any directions, you could ask them when rehearsals ended. He told actors exactly where they were to move, what gestures or stage business they should employ, and how the dialogue was to be timed. He played no favorites and treated stars, minor players, bit players and chorus in the same manner. He was courteous but impersonal, and he was perhaps the most successful stage director in the history of the American theater.

When I worked for Mr. Abbott, I had very little experience. I thought all directors worked as he did. I later learned that this was not so.

These were the days of live television. Each *Showcase* featured a major entertainment star and a young, emerging talent. Gordon Jenkins had assembled a core group of singers and dancers who sang, played in comedy sketches, danced in production numbers and occasionally appeared in commercials. Everyone in the group had Broadway experience – except for me. Mr. Abbott decided what was to be performed and staged the show. We rehearsed for five days, and on Sunday at 7:00 PM we went on the air. No video tape, no re-takes, and hopefully no mistakes. I badly wanted to succeed.

Among the stars that appeared on the *Showcase* were Bert Lahr, Rosemary Clooney, Joel Grey, Harpo Marx, Milton Berle, Kaye Ballard, Fred Allen, Beatrice Lillie, Jack Carson, Kathryn Grayson, Patricia Morison, Victor Borge, Louis Armstrong, and John Raitt. I remembered Joe's advice. I watched everything and learned.

In one *Showcase*, Ezio Pinza was the primary guest. He had been a major star of the Metropolitan Opera for many years before appearing on Broadway in Rodgers and Hammerstein's *South Pacific*. The *Showcase* writers created a scene with Pinza as a village blacksmith and I was cast as his assistant. The scene was a church picnic and we sang a traditional hymn - Pinza singing bass and me singing tenor.

His voice had lost little of its resonant power. I tried to blend, but I felt like young and light weight. The soprano was the German singer Hilda Geudden.

I had another connection to a *Showcase* guest. My parents were visiting and attended a rehearsal when Leo Durocher, colorful manager of baseball's New York Giants, was a guest. During a rehearsal break, my father spoke to him, recalling a game in the Georgia minor league. Attempting to steal third base, Durocher had been called out and flew into a rage "That was 35 years ago and I remember that play," my father said, "because I was the umpire, and I called you out!"

"You were wrong." Durocher shouted, leaping to his feet. "You were wrong and I was safe, I tell 'ya, safe!" And he smiled at the memory.

My father treasured that exchange for years to come.

The *Showcase* lasted for 26 weeks. Shortly after it went off the air, Gordon hired me again, this time for a recording date. I was told to report to Liederkrantz Hall on Manhattan's East side. The featured singer was recording star Peggy Lee, the song was *Lover,* by Richard Rodgers and Lorenz Hart. Gordon had fashioned an extravagant arrangement, with strings, woodwinds and three young, hyperkinetic bongo/conga players. I was to be Ms. Lee's 'phantom lover' - a voice in the background.

We rehearsed for some time, then the recording commenced. There was immediate trouble. The microphone arrangement wasn't balanced, then there were copying mistakes in the instrumental parts, then the lights were too glaring, then the 'bongo boys' didn't understand English instructions. In addition, Ms. Lee didn't like her monitor. An hour passed. Stop and start. Then more problems cropped up. Ms. Lee was getting very nervous and tense. It was a large studio, a converted community hall and occasional church, but in spite of the spaces I could feel the tension. Everyone became quiet. Another hour passed.

Then Gordon called a break. He and Ms Lee went out for a drink.

When they returned the microphone placement had been changed, the lights dimmed, a translator had arrived to help communicate with the bongo boys. Recording could resume. Most important, Ms. Lee was now relaxed and in a good mood. Now everything went smoothly.

When I could get Gordon's attention I asked, "What happened?" "Three martinis," Gordon whispered.

The recording was a huge commercial hit and Gordon and Ms. Lee added to their catalogue of successes. Decca also made a lot of money. It was an eerie feeling to walk through the theater district and hear the sound of my own voice coming from every bar and record shop.

After we wrapped the recording, Gordon talked about my singing. He suggested I might have a good career if I focused on pop songs and put aside 'the classical stuff.' He offered to help me. A wiser performer would have jumped at such an invitation, but I wasn't very wise. Or maybe I thought I knew everything about the music business. Whatever the reason, I was committed to a life in classical music and didn't follow his advice. Looking back, I think perhaps I made a big mistake.

Now, at the Smithsonian Museum of History and Technology, the history of popular culture was becoming relevant. Carl Scheele, head of the Division of Community Life, and Ellen Roney Hughes, museum specialist, began collecting and exhibiting popular culture artifacts. In their collection of sheet music was a copy of *Lover*. Among the other collections were the iconic chairs of Archie and Edith Bunker – well known set pieces from the television series *All In The Family*. And there was a collection of popular film objects, including the ruby slippers worn by Dorothy in *The Wizard of Oz*.

It seemed natural for Performing Arts to begin companion programs. For some time the world had been singing American songs, playing American music, watching American movies and television shows, enjoying American musical theater, wearing American style clothes – even experimenting with American style drugs. It was American popular culture that made the twenties roar, the thirties depressed, the forties swing and the fifties rock and roll.

It was also popular culture that in, 1969, gave the world the Woodstock Music Festival. This seminal event combined pop music, sex and drugs, in an announcement that popular culture was indeed a force to be recognized. Artifacts from the Woodstock Festival are now part of the collection of the National Museum of American History.

♩♩♩

I was surprised and delighted when Assistant Secretary Warner made a timely appointment. He hired Julian Euell as deputy assistant secretary. I thought Willie had made a wise decision. Julian brought a different, much needed depth of knowledge and experience to the Smithsonian. He was an

Afro-American and brought a different world view – one that the Smithsonian was often unable to use.

I was careful about booking popular culture programs. Assistant Secretary William Warner had pulled my coat, a pop culture phrase meaning he got my attention. urging me to be careful in popular culture programming. Willie's message went to the Smithsonian's–and particularly Secretary Dillon Ripley's–history of popular culture encounters.

When the Smithsonian Resident Associate Program presented a reading by Allen Ginsburg, poet-laureate of The Beat Generation, Ginsburg's speech attacked the CIA. Perhaps he didn't know, or remember that Ripley was a war-time member of the OSS – precursor of the CIA, and that he maintained close relationships with various CIA officials. The result was an order from Ripley prohibiting the booking of any more "contemporary novelists or poets."

The same fate befell New York Times film critic Pauline Kael when an invitation to lecture on modern films was withdrawn on Ripley's order. And a speaking invitation to poet Nikki Giovanni was also withdrawn.

Some time later the Resident Associates Program invited best-selling novelist and poet Erica Jong to lecture. In Jong's popular book, *Fear of Flying*, the author has her heroine describing her preference for "a zipless fuck."

Ripley ordered the invitation to Ms. Jong withdrawn. The American Civil Liberties Union sued the Smithsonian on behalf of Ms. Jong, and there was a settlement. Several days later Ripley called staff members and inquired, "What *is* a zipless fuck?" By now I had learned that such questions could be disingenuous, and I didn't respond.

So I respected Willie's advice and steered clear of controversial presentations. Instead, the Division of Performing Arts first foray into popular culture programming was a series of jazz concerts.

From the beginning, I wanted a jazz presence at the Smithsonian. Jazz was the supreme example of a popular culture creation that had developed into a world-class art form. It was music rooted in the Afro-American experience, and I thought jazz presentations would lend credibility to our goal of presenting overlooked and ignored aspects of American culture. I also thought we might begin to bridge the Smithsonian's problems with race.

I had made several attempts to program jazz performances. Beginning in 1967 I had requested funds to pay for a number of jazz concerts. I wanted to offer these concerts to the public free of charge. My appeal quoted composer and critic Virgil Thomson saying, "jazz is the most astounding spontaneous musical event to take place anywhere since the Reformation." I believe jazz may be America's unique contribution to the arts, and I quoted jazz scholar Martin Williams saying, "Jazz is the most respected Afro-American idiom, the most highly developed one, and the idiom to which improvisation is crucially important." No money was appropriated.

To understand the deeper social meanings of the music of black Americans was a task beyond my capabilities. But I believed institutions like the Smithsonian, where the arts of many cultures are preserved, studied and explained, had a huge responsibility – and a huge opportunity – to address the subject.

Frustrated by the decision, I formed a partnership with a group of young Washington jazz fans known as The Left Bank Jazz Society. The Smithsonian provided the Museum of Natural History's Baird Auditorium as a venue – free of charge. The LBJS booked the artists, sold tickets to cover artist's fees, and assumed all the risk.

The Smithsonian/Left Bank Jazz concerts began with Donald Byrd, followed by Benny Powell, Max Roach, McCoy Tyner, Art Blakey's Jazz Messengers and Roy Haynes. Our arrangement continued for several years, as my annual requests for jazz funding were denied.

Baird Auditorium seated 500 people, and the jazz concerts played to capacity audiences. It was not an ideal location. Lighting was poor, it was designed as a lecture hall and the acoustics were compromised. There were two small dressing rooms—only one with a functioning toilet, the other a storeroom for janitorial supplies. Requests for modifications were turned down, with claims that Secretary Ripley would not approve any changes.

I spoke to Ripley. He denied ever withholding approval for changes to Baird. We identified an acoustic expert who designed a floating ceiling over the stage, vastly improving the sound from the stage. Lighting positions were built and controls installed. The dressing rooms were up-dated, and Baird remains one of the best venues for musical performances in Washington.

The first predominately black audiences in Smithsonian history approached the museum warily, like entering foreign territory. But they were into the music. They listened and responded, at first with murmurs of approval, then with shouts of 'yeah,' or 'all right.' I savored this dialogue between artist and audience, and listened with a feeling of wonder. In the printed program I was listed as Director of Performing Arts, but at these performances I was always a student, always learning.

In 1969/70 I submitted yet another request, proposing to use Bicentennial Celebration funds to hire a full time jazz scholar. I was surprised and delighted when this time the request was approved.

I turned to Julian and others for advice in hiring a jazz expert. I remembered the carping about Ralph's credentials, and thought a jazz program needed a verifiable scholar. The best candidate was Martin Williams. He was widely respected and regarded by many as the finest American jazz journalist and critic. He had written for *The New York Times* and *Saturday Review*, co-founded of *The Jazz Review*, and was author of *The Art of Jazz, Jazz Panorama* and *Where's the Melody*. And Martin had also written provocative articles about popular culture.

Martin's interview went well and he was hired. I asked him to program our series of jazz concerts, and, most significantly, to develop a comprehensive list of jazz recordings with an eye toward a jazz record collection. We agreed that the selection of performances to be included would be subjective – the choices and opinions of one person. After lengthy conversations I was comfortable with the selection of Martin as that person.

I kept several of those 9¾ X 7½ cardboard backed composition books that are familiar to every student. I used the books to keep notes, articles, ideas, random thoughts, references and miscellany related to my Smithsonian job. One book was filled with information about jazz. I had saved scholarly articles, book reviews, record reviews, performance reviews, personality profiles, radio and television programs, films, gossip − anything that could shed light on the music and the musicians involved.

My accumulated bits and pieces showed that the history of jazz artists' creativity was documented on sound recordings, and these recordings were the property of more than 20 individual record companies. So it would be difficult for a student of this music to make an orderly study of its development. That led to an idea. Could the Smithsonian dare act as arbiter? Could we take the role of a national non-profit cultural center and convince record companies to lend selected items from their archives so that a comprehensive history of jazz performances could be assembled?

The beginning of a jazz program would be a watershed—a defining moment in my life and in the life of the Smithsonian's Division of Performing Arts.

I had been tasked with enlivening the Smithsonian museum and the Mall. With this new initiative the organization that I led would now move from booking agency to the practice of scholarship. I was not completely comfortable with the change. I never thought of myself as an expert or scholar. But I had been taught to listen. I had heard and performed a lot of music, and I did support the work of experts. And I did push for scholarly standards in the selection and annotation of programs. I had also urged Ralph to look for an opportunity, or a subject, that would yield a scholarly publication in the field of folk culture. I was also determined to seek out lesser known and under-appreciated American performing arts genres.

In all my endeavors I was grateful for the support of Assistant Secretary William Warner and Deputy Assistant Secretary Julian Euell, and for the staff I had assembled. It was a remarkable group. They were passionate about their work. They cared deeply about our emerging mission to recognize and celebrate overlooked American cultural achievements. I believed in a management style that shared decision making, with everyone empowered to participate and voice their opinion. I thought that all of us, together, were more effective than any one of us. The result was good morale, a strong degree of commitment and great productivity.

♬♬♬

Meanwhile, the 1970 Folklife Festival demanded attention. It was to feature the State of Arkansas and our first presentation of Native American cultures. In addition to the Arkansas participants, the Mall came alive with Portuguese-American fado musicians, Chinese dragon dancers, Eastern European singers and Spanish, Irish and Scottish bagpipers.

Arkansan Jimmy Driftwood was a popular attraction. His singing, guitar playing, fiddling and tale-telling gave evidence of his years as a teacher and song writer. In addition there were southern blues singers, ballad singers, bluegrass musicians and shouts and spirituals and jubilees. I stood with Jimmy Driftwood as un-accompanied ballad singer Almeda Riddle sang the classic ballad The House Carpenter. The song was one of the English and Scottish ballads collected in the

97

United States by Francis James Child and published in 10 volumes in 1884. Almeda sang slowly, verse after verse, recounting the epic tale of infidelity. When she got to the 10th or 11th verse, I turned to Jimmy with a quizzical look. "She's just getting started," he said. "I've heard her sing a hundred verses."

The Native American presentation featured Plains tribes and an evening pow-wow, with several hundred Native American dancers turning the Mall into a glorious sight. The Park Service estimated an attendance of 650,000 people.

Unlike the beginning years, Secretary Ripley now made it an essential part of his summer plans to be in Washington during the Festival. The Smithsonian acquired, for entertainment purposes, an elaborate *shamiana*, or Indian ceremonial tent shelter. Fabricated with exquisite, colorful, designs and ornate adornments, it would have been used in its homeland for weddings, receptions and ceremonial occasions. The Smithsonian shamiana, seating more than 100 guests, was erected on the roof terrace of the Museum of History and Technology, overlooking the Festival site and the July 4 fireworks display. It provided an elegant setting for Ripley's summer parties, with a guest list of celebrities and nabobs. And the lean Festival budget could only allow a $100 honorary payment to participants.

In the fall, the National Endowment for the Arts asked the Division of Performing Arts (via a letter to Martin and me) to host a national conference on jazz. Their request pointed out that we were the only established non-profit site in the Capital where the music could be heard. Martin and I assembled a group of scholars, critics and funding sources.

Participating musicians included Freddie Hubbard, Dizzy Gillespie, Hank Mobley, Betty Carter and our friends, The Left Bank Jazz Society. For two days we discussed the needs, desires and hopes of those who cared about this quintessential American music. These discussions led to the formation of the national endowment's Jazz Program.

Among the other under-appreciated American art forms that commanded attention was dance. Working at the New York City Center Opera Company in the 1950s I came to know Charles Weidman, and later Pearl Lang. Weidman was one of the founders of a dance style "that sprang from American soil." With contemporaries Doris Humphrey, Ruth St. Denis, Martha Graham, Alwin Nickolais and others, they created a dance style and vocabulary of movement that changed the way the world danced. They called it simply American Modern Dance.

Weidman was revered as a choreographer, dancer and teacher of Gene Kelly, Jack Cole, Bob Fosse, Alvin Ailey and others. He was a kind and gentle man, and rather shy. He was generous with his thoughts and advice, and he taught me about the inter-relationship between dance and other performing genres. Weidman was deeply concerned that recognition be given to those who desired to express, in dance, something of the time in which we lived.

"It was a time of great cultural change, where innovation was occurring in all the arts." Weidman said. I was reminded again that to know and appreciate our culture, America should have a museum of the performing arts. In the absence of such a place, I believed the Smithsonian should have a role here, that the institution could perform a vital function.

I wanted to showcase dance creativity as it was happening. Charles Reinhart, director of the American Dance Festival, gave good advice, and I arranged performances by Twyla Tharp, Paul Sanasardo, Meredith Monk and Yvonne Rainer. I was inspired by Ms. Tharp, but canceled her performance when she became pregnant. Sanasardo's performance grew out of a new approach to traditional ballet and was spiritual. Meredith Monk recruited 30 local non-dance students and created a work called *Museum Dance*. The work took place at various locations throughout the Museum of Natural History, and was a success with audience and critics.

During this time there were nation-wide protests against the war in Vietnam. There were demonstrations on the streets, at public spaces – anywhere that would draw attention to the cause. National Guard Troops, sent to restore order at Kent State University, fired on a group of young activists, killing two and wounding others. Protests occurred across the country, in solidarity with the students.

In Washington, police attacked protesters, who often used the rotunda of the National Archives, across the Mall, as sanctuary.

During this time, the Smithsonian sponsored a National Symposium entitled *Contemporary Changes Affecting Man's Sense of Social Identity*. I was asked to contribute a paper on the subject, Contemporary Changes in the Arts. Rather than submit a paper I invited modern dance pioneer and peace activist Yvonne Rainer to perform. Supplementing Rainer's appearance was *The Electric Stereopticon* performing music by John Cage, Paul Steg and Lejaren Hiller. Kenneth Gaburo's New Music Choral Ensemble performed, and we presented electronic music compositions by Morton Subotnic and Loren Carrier.

Ms. Rainer planned to perform in the Museum of History and Technology Flag Hall, where the original Star Spangled Banner was displayed. Several days before her performance she showed me an excerpt from her dance.

We met in our conference room. She shut the door, then removed all of her clothes. She stood naked for several moments, then she took an American flag from an overnight bag she had brought. Using the flag as a prop, she began to move, sensuously. She used the flag-now as a shawl, then as a head scarf, then around her bare body, then between her legs, in a gesture familiar to burlesque fans. Her moves were not provocative, but graceful, with no hint of self-consciousness.

My first reaction was to try and stay cool. I breathed deeply and tried to relax. My 'cool' evaporated when someone knocked on the conference room door and tried to enter. It was my secretary, asking if I wanted a sandwich for lunch. I blocked the door, asked the intruder to go away. Now it was me who was self-conscious. Finally I asked Rainer to get dressed. She took her time in responding. I had to decide on a proper reaction to her proposed performance. I didn't think I had a choice, and said there would be no nude flag dance performed in a Smithsonian museum. She must have known I would deny her request. Denied, she went public with the story, alerting all the media.

On the evening of the performance, Yvonne Rainer and Group performed a 70 minute-dance narrative, clothed. The dance contained numerous visual and verbal protests of U. S. foreign policy and the Vietnam War. Her protests were artful. The audience had waited in anticipation of a dramatic confrontation. They were disappointed. .

In a public interview after her performance, I was challenged by the press. Did the Smithsonian have an official policy regarding the war in Vietnam? No. Did the Smithsonian believe in censoring artists? No. Was Ms. Rainer an artist? Yes. Since a recent museum art exhibition had included famous nude paintings and had not been censored, would I explain why the exhibited nudes were ok and Rainer's live nude performance was censored? No.

In a final statement I said Ms. Rainer had been hired on the basis of her previous work. I said she declined to work from her prior base and elected instead to make a new work, incorporating a political statement. I said I believed she had breached our agreement.

The evening ended quietly. It was a very odd experience for me. I didn't believe in censoring artists. And I shared her objections to the administration's actions.

The Rainer performance occurred as scheduled. Her actions generated unnecessary stress. It also brought criticism of me from Smithsonian management. Nevertheless, I believed the idea that the national museum might provide a continuing survey of new arts endeavors was valid. The criticism was tempered by an article by *Washington Post* critic Alan Kreigsman congratulating the Smithsonian on "esthetic risk taking and bringing provocative, radical and stimulating visions to Washington audiences."

TEN

Jazz, Outreach and Conflict

The 1971 Folklife Festival featured the State of Ohio, with ragtime and Cajun music, Caribbean music and dance, rhythm and blues and rock and roll.

Ralph and I discussed his political concerns and his resignation. I opposed American involvement in Vietnam, but did not think his protest would influence anyone.. He didn't argue, and a few hours later he withdrew his resignation.

I flew to Columbus, Ohio, to attend a luncheon at the Governor's Mansion. Some 60 political and business leaders were gathered to hear about an Ohio participation in the Folklife Festival. I made a 25-minute speech about the Smithsonian, the Festival and traditional culture in Ohio. At the conclusion of my speech the governor announced the title of the Ohio participation would be 'A Partnership for People.' The entire Ohio participation cost was raised in less than 30 minutes.

We contracted with Mack McCormick to supplement Ralph's field research, and both did an excellent job. The work styles and crafts of structural and ornamental iron workers was another step toward a 'folklife' presentation. Demonstrations by meat cutters, butchers, bakers and confectionary workers was a beginning involvement with union members. Mack found the son of deceased blues legend Robert Johnson living in Cleveland and playing his fathers music. The colorful culture on Northwest Coast Native Americans added to a very good festival.

The 1971 Festival also generated some prophetic controversy when the selection of another blues musician - a young black man – turned out to be a mistake, at least in my judgment. His playing was out of tune and inept. Compared to the standard set by other musicians on the program, there were questions about our participant selection process. The incident was embarrassing for Festival staff – and I believe the young man was also embarrassed.

Deputy Assistant Secretary Julian Euell and recently hired jazz scholar Martin Williams were both present for the performance. Julian expressed his concern to Ralph, saying the selection of an inferior black artist revealed an element of condescending racism. Martin's comments were even stronger. He felt the selection of a third-rate black musician denigrated the achievements of both black and white artists. Martin also argued that some folklorists were beset by a 'Marxist' attitude, one that venerated the proletariat - working class society. He saw this attitude as a need by some to look down on a social class, leading to the championing and manipulation of that class.

The ensuing argument angered Ralph, who claimed that Julian and Martin didn't understand that the musician in question was 'of his community.' Martin belittled Ralph's argument. We needed a time out.

The argument cooled after some time, but the attitudes survived and created a continuing strain. I shared Julian's concerns, but questioned the existence of hidden racism in festival programming. I didn't agree with Martin's 'Marxist' accusations, and I thought he was bating Ralph, but his view was shared by some politicians, social historians and critics.

$$\text{♮♮♮}$$

We returned to the office to find a proposal from the 'VISIT U.S.A.' division of the U. S. Department of Commerce. They intended a return to Montreal, Canada, site of Expo 67, and occupation of the fabled USA/Expo pavilion, Buckminster Fuller's geodesic dome. The DOC objective was to promote tourism and they asked the Smithsonian to produce a version of the Folklife Festival in Canada.

The DOC proposal sparked an intense debate within the Smithsonian. Those in favor argued that income from the contract would help pay for planned Smithsonian expansions, and for future festivals. Others welcomed the idea as an example of Smithsonian outreach - a priority at the time. Those opposed cited lack of trained staff and a strain on resources. I was in favor. Ralph was opposed.

Previously I had supported Ralph's authority as Festival Director but he was too busy to add a Montreal event to his schedule. A DOC contract would mean finding someone else to do the research and programming. Finally, money and outreach were the deciding factors. We agreed to proceed, with Mack McCormick as program director.

Mack and I met in Montreal, on a bitterly cold day, the thermometer at seven degrees Fahrenheit. Fuller's dome was recognized as an inspired piece of architectural design. We wondered if the awesome building would overpower the modest scale of folk musicians and crafters.

**Buckminster Fuller geodesic dome,
U.S. Pavilion, Expo 67, Montreal, Canada**

I needed to imagine the space filled with the sound of traditional crafters, musicians and singers because DOC sent me around the United States to describe the program we would present. Each VISIT USA region controlled their portion of DOC's promotional budget. In Atlanta, Georgia, I spoke to a gathering of travel representatives from the southeastern region. In Baltimore, it was representatives from the mid-Atlantic region. In Boston, it was reps from the northeast region, mid-west reps in Chicago, Pacific area reps in San Francisco, northwest reps in Seattle, southwest reps in Dallas – a lot of traveling and talking. Every speech was covered by the press.

In the beginning I used a canned speech, but discarded it in favor of a photo slide show followed by questions and answers. The answers required improvising, explaining the folklife festival idea, describing how participants would be identified with regions, and characterizing the Smithsonian Institution's role as folk culture presenter. In the end, every one of the regions agreed to participate. And the Smithsonian got a lot of outreach.

The Montreal dome stood some twenty stories high. Visitors would enter and proceed to multi-level platforms connected by escalators and walkways. A mini-rail system carried passengers through the building and to other sites on the exposition grounds.

Whatever we produced would necessarily be compared with the hugely popular success of Expo 67. It was a risky proposition, and a public failure might have had a negative impact on the Washington Festival.

The VISIT USA exhibition opened in mid-June and continued for 13 weeks. Two members of our Washington staff, Mary Carrington and Diane Ziler, were detailed to manage travel and logistics and their contributions were invaluable.

Mack organized a strong program that changed each week. Some participants were Folklife Festival veterans, others new to Festival performances. Additions included new crafts people, Grand Ole Opry star Roy Acuff, jazz pianist Teddy Wilson, blues pianist Roosevelt Sykes, Duke Ellington veteran Ray Nance, Jay McShann and his Kansas City Jazz Band (the band that had included Charlie Parker and Lester Young), Bill Danoff and Taffy Nivert, (co-authors of *Take Me Home, Country Roads,*) the powerful blues singer Jimmy Witherspoon and many others.

VISIT USA concluded with a tribute to ragtime music, spotlighting the cities where the music was born and developed. Throughout the summer I commuted between Washington and Montreal, studying program management and logistics of a changing weekly festival. Ralph was also a frequent visitor. It was great experience, valuable in planning the Smithsonian's twelve-week Bicentennial Festival. The DOC reported that VISIT USA was a success, and met their goals.

In the fall Ralph called and asked for a private talk. We met at a park on the Potomac River, where I had docked a small sailing boat. We talked for hours. He was unhappy and concerned about Julian and Martin's reaction to his program choices, and he was anxious about my involvement in activities other than the Folklife Festival. He said he believed the success of the festival was due to my leadership, our ability to work together as a team and our friendship and feeling of trust. He was frustrated with government procedures and afraid I was losing interest in the festival.

I assured him that I supported his efforts and my first priority was the Festival of American Folklife. I hoped my responses quieted his anxieties.

Fall programs continued with a benefit concert featuring American soprano Jessye Norman, the Tehcheng Shadow Puppet Theater from China, the Saeko Dance Ensemble from Japan, and another season of children's programs in a new Discovery Theater.

Jazz Heritage concerts included Lee Konitz, Ornette Coleman, the Modern Jazz Quartet, the Thad Jones and Mel Lewis Big Band, Sonny Rollins and a ragtime concert featuring Gunther Schuller.

During this period we enjoyed strong public support for our programs, but not everything we attempted was successful. The history of American theater and entertainment was of interest to the popular culture curators. And it was a matter of personal interest to me – I had worked in the vineyards of Dionysus, the God of theater, for many years. A contact with Caedmon Records, the pioneers in spoken word recordings, revealed a mutual interest in American theater history. I proposed recording seminal American plays, performed by star actors, directed by the best stage directors and packaged with educational materials.

A survey of educators, actors and directors revealed strong interest in the venture. The first plays would be *The Contrast* by Royall Tyler; *Metamora* by John Augustus Stone; *Uncle Tom's Cabin* adapted by George Baker, *The Faith Healer* by William Vaughn Moody; *Of Mice and Men* by John Steinbeck; *Fashion* by Anna Cora Mowatt; and *Our Town* by

Thornton Wilder, plus excerpts from minstrel shows, revues and musical theater.

We believed the recorded works would generate interest in the museum's collections of entertainment history items, so I was disappointed when Caedmon had money problems that forced their withdrawal. The venture was abandoned, and with it, my best hope of a beginning to theater research.

It was gratifying when our enlivening endeavors got the attention of other museums, colleges and universities, and when hey asked to share our programs. The requests meshed with a new Smithsonian emphasis on outreach. The emphasis was not egalitarian but a reaction to complaints that the Smithsonian was, in fact, a Washington institution, not a national enterprise.

I responded to the requests by creating the Smithsonian Touring Performance Service, packaging programs we presented in Washington and sending them out to regional and local presenters. Children's Theater performances and ethnic musical artists were popular. The most in-demand performance was a program about Afro-American culture, featuring Bernice Reagan. The program spoke to a growing need for multi-cultural attractions, a need that was not being met by other museums, colleges of universities – and by commercial presenters.

The Touring Performances Service functioned successfully for ten years, until commercial producers picked up the model and fed a developing need for educational and socially aware programming.

In the early months of 1972 we began work on the next Folklife Festival. The featured state was Maryland, with examples of horse culture, the ways of Chesapeake watermen, colorful and exciting ethnic performers and Baltimore street life. A historic skipjack, one of the Chesapeake sailing ships used by commercial fisheries, sailed up the Potomac River and docked near the Jefferson Memorial. A track was laid out on the Mall and Maryland thoroughbreds raced. Carpenters and joiners demonstrated their skills and 'arabers' – Baltimore venders with horse drawn fruit and vegetable carts plied the festival grounds.

Lithographers and photoengravers, sponsored by their unions, introduced a curious and fascinated audience to the present-day versions of ancient printing techniques. The Maryland presentation was well researched and produced, but torrential rain storms flooded the Mall and the adjacent waterways. The drenched participants endured, as did the audience.

ELEVEN

The Smithsonian Collection of Recordings

James Smithson's gift to the United States-105 bags of British gold sovereigns-was to be used for "the increase and diffusion of knowledge." Smithson's generous gift left the specifics to future generations.

Secretary Ripley's assignment to me was the enlivenment of the museums and their collections. That assignment was amended to read "and address aspects of American culture generally overlooked in museums." Those last words signaled a very big change in my mission. A major overlooked aspect of American culture was the creation of an original and unique American musical form known as jazz.

When jazz historian and scholar Martin Williams joined our staff his assignment was to help create a basic survey of teaching resources by major artists involved in the development of that music. In his annual Smithsonian Year Report, Ripley wrote, "the phonograph record provides us with a unique opportunity to preserve an aural past that otherwise would have been lost. They also give us the means of hearing jazz played by the very musicians and singers who created the music and built its history."

In 1973 the publication of *The Smithsonian Collection of Classic Jazz* was released. The chosen recordings were owned by more than fifteen companies, and stored in their archives. Obtaining rights to use these recordings was the fulfillment of a dream.

I suggested we ask the record companies for permission to incorporate their archival recordings. Martin had carefully identified the recordings we wanted to use, and I was frankly amazed when a majority agreed. Their cooperation in a project of this kind was literally - unprecedented.

It was Martin Williams' idea that we approach W. W. Norton Publishing Company, a leading publisher of books on music. We suggested that Norton might use *Classic Jazz* as a supplement to their widely used music history text books. I was delighted when Norton agreed, and even more delighted when they purchased the first 10,000 copies of *Classic Jazz*.

With text, recorded lists, record company releases and Norton's purchasing agreement in hand, I asked the Smithsonian treasurer for permission to buy additional copies of *Classic Jazz* to sell to associate members and the general public. "We're not in the record business" was the reply. We argued that recordings were a legitimate form of publication, and not unlike issues by the Smithsonian Press. Finally the treasurer agreed to a purchase of 100 copies for re-sale.

Advance copies of *Classic Jazz* were sent to a handful of writers and critics, many of whom were Martin's former colleagues. A few weeks later Whitney Bailliet, jazz critic for *the New Yorker Magazine*, wrote the first review, saying,

"Here, at last, is a comprehensive history of jazz performances. *The Smithsonian Collection of Classic Jazz* is a breakthrough in jazz history. For the first time it's possible to survey the pinnacles of the music, and what a panorama it is."

The *Music Educators Journal* followed, calling it "A major accomplishment....an immense contribution."

Jazz critic Nat Hentoff wrote, "An extraordinary accomplishment. I doubt if there will be a bigger bargain for a long time. The accompanying book is a remarkably penetrating brief history of jazz."

Equally enthusiastic reviews followed in the *New York Times*, the *Chicago Tribune*, the *Los Angeles Times* and numerous other newspapers. *Time* and *Newsweek* echoed the praise. And every review concluded: For additional information contact the Smithsonian's Division of Performing Arts.

It's a lovely feeling to have achieved a major goal. There's no question that the sun shines brighter, the flowers smell sweeter, and adversaries are confounded.

The good reviews rolled in and the orders rolled out. The office mail usually arrived in the postman's shoulder bag. Now the mail arrived in large, cardboard boxes. Envelopes came with checks, cash, stamps and money orders to purchase *Classic Jazz*, and our supply of 100 copies was exhausted in hours.

A call to W. W. Norton convinced them to sell back some of their purchased inventory. A rented truck was dispatched to retrieve several thousand copies. The astonished Treasurer quickly approved a second pressing, then several more. We had no fulfillment service, so part of each day was spent with Performing Arts staff wrapping *Classic Jazz* packages in brown paper and hand addressing each package. The parcels were then hauled to the Post Office in my automobile. A person from the Accounting Office was detailed to count the receipts and make daily bank deposits. A planned advertisement ran in *Smithsonian Magazine,* adding to the flow of orders. In desperation we contracted a fulfillment service to handle the purchases, and in a matter of weeks we were the proprietors of a booming business.

The Smithsonian Collection of Classic Jazz, boxed set recording

118

And irony abounded! What was expected was not what occurred. By years' end, sales of *Classic Jazz* had exceeded our expectations. The treasurer, who said we were 'not in the record business,' called to suggest we were, after all, in the record business. He also suggested I think of other recording packages that might sell. In response to his suggestions, we packaged. a compilation of Bach trio sonatas with a recording of the Brandenburg Concertos. We called the package the *Smithsonian Collection of Classic Bach*. The sales were quite good.

The National Endowment for the Arts (NEA) gave our office a grant to establish a jazz oral history project. Martin Williams was to supervise and he selected a young jazz scholar named J. R. Taylor to accumulate the interviews. I soon came to admire Taylor's acumen and insights. The NEA also solicited our advice on the use of recordings to stimulate national interest in other forms of music. Then the Music Critics Association asked us to train music critics to write knowledgeably about more than the standard musical literature. Martin taught a series of seminars on jazz writing; I taught on writing popular song criticism.

I congratulated Martin on his accomplishment and he congratulated me on my idea for publishing a jazz history. He compiled more recordings, off-shoots of *Classic Jazz* and archival reconstructions of Broadway musicals, beginning with a Victor Herbert collection. He also encouraged conductor and music historian Gunther Schuller's work to notate and publish musical scores of jazz compositions. Schuller would often travel with a portable record player and a supply of discs. Working in a hotel room, between performances, he laboriously notated what he heard.

Meanwhile, the 1973 Folklife Festival featured the State of Kentucky and Northern Plains Indians. New themes were introduced, as Ralph coined the phrase, 'Old Ways in the New World,' bringing together Croatian and Serbian performers from Yugoslavia with their American counterparts. Their eastern-European music was powerful and rich, with dissonant harmonies and forceful rhythms. They shared their traditions with second and third generation offspring, families from the eastern region of Pennsylvania. In addition, an 'Old Ways' program explored English ballad traditions that were still alive in American communities.

Aided by labor historian and folklorist Archie Green, we created a Working American's theme that featured union members and the culture of the building trades.

And we seized opportunities to present other types of music.

In 1969, ground was broken for a new museum on the National Mall. After a personal campaign by Secretary Ripley and President Lyndon Johnson, wealthy art collector and patron Joseph Hirshhorn gave funds, plus his collection of modern art and sculpture, to the Smithsonian Institution. It was a great move, and an example of the vision that was Ripley's greatest attribute. With the Hirshhorn Museum and Sculpture Garden open, I recommended the inclusion of contemporary music in their program plans. Although the museum director wasn't particularly enthusiastic, he didn't oppose the idea.

We had previously programmed works by George Rothberg, George Crumb, Arnold Schoenberg, Olivier Messian, Steve Reich, Charles Ives and others. Then, in 1978, Jim Weaver recommended we adopt the 20th Century Consort (now the 21st Century Consort) as the Hirshhorn's resident ensemble. Producer Anthony Ames, a National Symphony percussionist, and conductor Christopher Kendall had a good programming record. The Consort agreed, and we continued to pay due respect to contemporary music.

Programming contemporary music was like swimming upstream. The music lacked the immediate popular appeal of folk music and jazz and no one in the Institution, or the general public, gave a damn whether it was played or not. But I believed the music of our own time challenged our expectations. It allowed us to know an artist's view of life, beauty and art, and it questioned our ability to hear and think. I also believed that a museum would be the best of all environments for presenting and understanding contemporary music. We had loudly proclaimed that vital museums were about the often risky art of now, not the safe and sacrosanct art of yesterday.

Martin's recorded reconstructions of Broadway musicals added to our involvement with an important popular culture genre, and generated very good press. It also resuscitated my personal involvement with the American musical.

In 1955, Joe Moon's coaching studio was on the top floor of the Steinway Building, West 57th Street, New York City. He coached three days per week, with students ranging from established Broadway performers like Alfred Drake, Tom

Euell, Patricia Morison, Kitty Carlisle and Gertrude Lawrence, to aspiring young actors.

Previously, I had coached with Joe, off and on, for two years, learning the nuances of musical theater performance. We also became friends, and his son is named James Morris Moon. Now Joe asked me to sing some duets with an English actress he was coaching as she prepared auditions for a forthcoming show.

She was a lovely, 19-year-old, with porcelain-like complexion, a type often called an English Rose. We sang together several times-duets from musicals and a few classical pieces. She had a very good voice, a bright, clean sound, with a terrific range. We became friends and she came to our apartment for dinner. We had no dining room table, so we sat on the floor, ate and talked about our lives and hopes. We laughed that her mother's maiden name was also Morris. She was currently on Broadway in *The Boy Friend*, a British import, where she received very good reviews. Her name was Julie Andrews.

An acquaintance of Joe's, a society type, asked him to suggest two singers for an informal afternoon performance to benefit her favorite charity. Joe asked Julie and me if we would be interested - for fun - and we agreed.

Some 50 people were seated in the large, East-side duplex while Julie and I waited in the kitchen. Minutes before we were to sing I looked through the small butler's window and spotted three men, seated in the front row. From news photos I recognized Alan Lerner and Frederick Loewe, lyricist and composer of *Brigadoon* and *Paint Your Wagon*. The third person was Moss Hart, one of the theater's most successful writers and directors. Julie saw them and grew pale. They were creating a new show, she had auditioned, and they had come to hear her again.

The living room seats were quickly filled. Joe played the piano and Julie and I sang show duets like *If I Loved You* from Carousel and a classical duet by Henry Purcell. I thought we sang well, there was lots of applause, and the hostess was delighted with the money raised for her charity.

After our performance, Lerner and Loewe and Hart were very complimentary, and delighted with Julie. They also liked my singing, mentioned the new show they were assembling, and said there might be something for me in the show. At the time I was preparing for operatic appearances in *La Traviata* and *Andrea Chenier,* with contracts promised in the New Year, so I declined the offer and said I had other plans.

Six months later my 'other plans' had evaporated. With appropriate chagrin and sincere humility, I called the Lerner and Loewe office and pleaded for an audition.

The line from the Hellinger Theater stretched around the corner and up the adjacent block. It was reported that 600 singers had come for the original casting call, and the current line-up included 200 call-backs, for 16 jobs.

Eight at a time we sang our audition songs. I don't remember what I sang, but I was told to wait. Others in my group were sent home. The routine continued until 16 singers remained. Stage manager Samuel (Biff) Liff introduced himself, told us we were hired and passed out tax forms to sign. Someone asked the name of the show, and Liff replied, "That's still being discussed. It may be Lady Liza, or just Lisa."

The name that was finally chosen for Lerner and Loewe's show was *My Fair Lady*.

We gathered on January 3rd, 1956, in the roof garden theater of the New Amsterdam Theater on 42nd Street,. The cast, composer, writer, director, choreographer, stage managers, scenic and costume designers and the music director, all seated in a semi-circle around an upright piano. The composer and writer were to read and sing through the new musical show.

When it first opened, in 1903, the New Amsterdam was New York City's largest theater, seating 1800 people. Decorated in mauve, green and dull gold colors, it was called 'The House Beautiful,' and 'the most beautiful Art Nouveau theater in America'. By 1927 it had been home to 14 Ziegfeld Follies, shows that brought many of the countries greatest actors to its stage. This was where Leon Errol, Bert Williams, Fanny Brice, Will Rodgers, W. C. Fields and hundreds of the most beautiful women entertained delighted audiences.

In 1934 the New Amsterdam was closed and later re-opened as a movie theater. In 1993, Disney Theatrical Productions signed a 99-year lease on the property, and began a $34 million renovation. In 1997 the Disney production of *The Lion King* returned the historic venue to its rightful destiny as the home of great theater.

But in 1956 the New Amsterdam was in poor condition, its carpets worn and ragged, its acclaimed proscenium façade crumbling. An ancient elevator carried the actors up to the roof garden theater. When everyone was seated in rows, Moss Hart, the show's director, introduced Alan Lerner, the writer; Frederick (Fritz) Loewe, the composer. Then he introduced

Hayna Holm, the choreographer, Oliver Smith, the set designer, Cecil Beaton, the costume designer, and music director Franz Allers. Then Hart introduced the principle actors, beginning with Rex Harrison, who would play Henry Higgins, Julie Andrews, who would play Eliza Doolittle, Stanley Holloway as Alfred P. Doolittle, Robert Coote as Colonel Pickering, Cathleen Nesbitt as Mrs. Higgins, and Michael King as Freddie Eynsford-Hill.

There was the rustling sound of pages being turned, and Hart read the stage directions. In proper sequence, the actors read their parts.

Hart later remembered the leading actors gave 'a brilliant reading.' Loewe played the piano and Lerner talk/sang the songs as they occurred in the story. There was an air of joyful excitement. Cecil Beaton wrote in his diary, "....everyone was keyed up, convinced that they were participating in something exciting. Each song was spontaneously applauded. The air was electric."

I felt that electricity. I was hired to play a bit roll-one of the Loverly Quartet-and to sing in the ensemble. During the read-through I became keenly aware of the theatrical wonder that Lerner and Loewe had created, and their inspired choices of words and music. Scenes are beautifully constructed, the persona of each character captured in the writing. The flow of dialogue and music seemed natural, inevitable and seamless.

In the opening scene Henry Higgins asks, *Why Can't the English Teach their Children How to Speak?* and in one stroke, Lerner has captured the premise of George Bernard Shaw's play on which the musical is based. When Eliza sings, *Wouldn't it be Loverly?* we understand her yearning for a

125

better life and we share her triumph at the Embassy Ball, with *I Could Have Danced All Night*.

I knew Shaw's play, Pygmalion, in its 1938 movie version, with Leslie Howard and Wendy Hiller in the principal rolls. I loved the film and must have seen it a dozen or more times. I'd read the play, written in 1913, and reveled in Shaw's clever dialogue.

As rehearsals begin I watch Hart create characters, stage pictures and scenes that evolve in fluid action, and I'm reminded again of Lehman Engle's teaching.

In an off-stage dressing room, some of us are taught to speak like Cockneys by dialect specialist Alfred Dixon, while dancers learn moves and attitudes with Hayna Holm and the movements of principal actors are blocked by Moss Hart.

I watched Harrison work. He repeats details of stage business, he's meticulous, weighing words like jewels on an ordinal scale, synthesizing line readings with bits of action. Years later, in his autobiography, *A Damned Serious Business*, he wrote, "I've always tried to make my acting look very simple, as natural as possible, and as truthful...acting that never calls attention to itself is a difficult business. If it's done immaculately and looks as though it hasn't been any trouble, that's when it's been the most trouble. If it looks like a hell of a sweat, that's when it hasn't been taken care of very well."

It's reported that he's frustrated with Julie's habit of laughing at his lines, and he says, "If that bitch is here on Monday, I'm quitting the show." He's a tough guy to work with - demanding. He's not a singer, but he's working on a technique he calls sing/speak. In Germany they call it 'sprechstimme.'

As rehearsals proceed, there are reports that Julie is not doing well. 'Out of her depth,' someone says. Moss gives everyone time off while he works with her, line by line. "He made me infuriated," Julie remembers, "and scared, and mad and frightened and in awe and full of an inferiority complex. I didn't know what Eliza should be, a whiney girl or a gutsy girl - a weak character or a strong one."

Kitty Carlisle says she can hear Moss's inflections in Julie's line readings.

At the first reading, Julie ran to me and gave me a hug. I was happy to see her, and she seemed delighted that I was in the cast. Now she is removed, still with a warm smile, but distracted. But she is such a quick study-learning dance movements and musical details at once. Pitch perfect.

I've been assigned a minor role - 3rd Cockney in the opening scene - part of a quartet that backs Julie in *Wouldn't it be Loverly?* I have a nice solo, and am told I got the assignment because Fritz Loewe likes my voice.

Rehearsals continue. Now Julie has it! She's more relaxed, terrific, poised and confident. Everyone seems happy, looking forward to getting on stage.

The cast decamps to New Haven, and the first rehearsals with orchestra. Julie, Stanley and Michael King have all sung with an orchestra, but this is new territory for Rex. The rhythmic flexibility of other rehearsals, when he sings with piano accompaniment, is gone - replaced by the sound of 32 instruments. Peter Howard, the rehearsal pianist, had emphasized Rex's musical cues. Now the cues are buried in the orchestra and he can't be sure of what he's hearing. He panics. His fear increases as the stage performances loom. Then, the afternoon before the first performance, Rex locks himself in his dressing room. He sends word. "I just can't open, I just cannot open... I refuse to go on."

I'm having an early dinner with several other cast members. We're at Kaysey's Restaurant, across the street from the Shubert Theater stage door. Bernie Hart, the assistant stage manager and Moss' brother, arrives with the news. We're all dumbfounded. Speechless.

No one can remember when, if ever, a show has been cancelled on opening night. That a star of Harrison's magnitude would lose his nerve is the stuff of rumors, but this is the real thing. The news comes in bits and pieces.

The Shubert organization owns the theater, and they're threatening to sue Harrison and the *My Fair Lady* producers. Rex's agent arrives and is shouting at him through the dressing room door, warning that he is jeopardizing his career. Lilli Palmer, his ex-wife, and Kay Kendall, his wife-to-be, are both there, trying to reason with him. A chartered plane is on its way, with alarmed executives from CBS who financed the show. Rumors have circulated that the show will be a huge hit, and trains full of people are on their way to see the first performance.

I've lost track of the hour. The crowd from Kaysey's is drifting over to the theater. We don't know where else to go, and we must learn what's happening. More time passes, until, at last, Bernie comes. He tells us to get into make-up. Rex has relented and we're to report for half-hour, as planned.

The curtain rises late - but that it rises at all is surprising. No one knows what to expect. If the nervous electricity in the theater could be captured it would power much of New England. The overture goes as planned. Now comes *Why Can't the English,* Rex's first number. Backstage is very quiet. Listening. How would it go? Would it go at all?

Rex is brilliant! Every line is delivered with ease and panache. He's relaxed and assured, the humorous words trigger explosions of laughter and applause, and the audience is given a lesson in the art of playing high comedy.

We hurry and change costumes for *With a Little Bit of Luck,* Stanley's first song. He's rousing, and the audience responds with an ovation. And so it goes, scene after scene, number after number.

Not everything is perfect. The large set pieces, designed for New York's Hellinger Theater, won't quite fit on the Shubert stage. The revolving turntables won't turn smoothly. Scene changes take longer than expected, scenes run longer than planned. And the final curtain doesn't fall till past midnight. But the audience doesn't seem to care. Julie is a delight. Sure in her line delivery, singing with charm and clarity. Stanley gives a performance of great wit and energy. And Rex? Rex's definition of Henry Higgins will become iconic.

The show is too long, and cuts must be made. One song, *Say a Prayer for Me Tonight* is cut and will end up in the movie, *Gigi.* A complicated dance number is dropped. The authors are not satisfied with Michael King's performance of *On the Street Where You Live.* Reid Shelton and I are called to audition as Michael's replacement. Reid is chosen. I'm told I sound "too mature and masculine." Reid plays the role for several performances. The authors are still not satisfied, and Michael is re-instated.

The show moves to the Erlanger Theater in Philadelphia for four more weeks of trials. The reviews are ecstatic, and the show is 'frozen.' No more changes.

And no more hotels. In Philly, I share an apartment with Lerner's assistant, Stone (Bud) Widney. Bud and I decide to throw a party, and Lerner, Loewe, Holloway, King, Hanya Holm, Franz Allers and most of the cast attend. Moss must be in New York. Rex does not attend.

A week later I get an urgent message. An assistant manager at the Metropolitan Opera has called my wife, inviting me to audition for the company. Someone on the Met staff has heard me in a performance with the First Opera Quintet, and they want to hear me 'in the house,' I'm very, very excited by the invitation.... and anxious.

Monday is a day off and I take a morning train to New York. I walk the few blocks, from Penn Station to the old opera house on 39th street. This is the Met's home before it moved to Lincoln Center. My mouth is dry. This is the theater where de Luca, Caruso , Tibbett, Bjoerling, Chaliapin, Tibaldi and so many others have performed.

I'm welcomed at the stage door, and told to wait. Now there's time to warm-up. Then I'm called to go onstage, and I'm walking over the battered stage floor, scarred with the fasteners of countless scenery anchors. Sitting at a piano on stage is a cool, somewhat disinterested accompanist. I tell him what I've decided to sing and offer the printed score. He waves the score away, with a gesture that says 'I've played those arias hundreds of times. I don't need the music.'

Out in the dark cavern of the theater I make out four ghost-like figures. I can't see their faces. One of the 'ghosts' speaks. "All right Mr. Morris, what will you sing?" I answer, "Traviata, the di provensa, and Chenier, the Nemico." The 'rehearsal-speak'- epithets, for Germond's aria from *La Traviata* and Gerard's aria from *Andrea Chenier* were common. I'm trying to be cool – nonchalant.

I mange to blot out the surroundings, push away my nerves. I sing fairly well, I think, but with some anxiety about my selections. The *Andrea Chenier* aria is usually sung by someone with a darker, heavier voice than mine, but it's dramatic, with opportunities to act the scene. I send a mental 'thanks' to Ernestine Perrie for her coaching. I finish, and wait while the 'ghosts' discuss my performance. I can't hear what they say. Then I hear, "Thank you, Mr. Morris." That's all, just "thank you."

I leave by the stage door and walk into the crowded streets of the garment district, passing men pushing carts hung with racks of coats and dresses. They exchange shouts and taunts, throwing an occasional "watch it' in my direction and I avoid a collision. I dive into the subway station at 40th street, ride uptown to meet my wife.

"How did it go?" she asks. I really don't know how it went. We go to dinner at a restaurant on 69th street, a familiar place where I know all the waiters and nod in response to their greetings. We don't mention the audition, try to talk about other things. In the morning I catch the train for Philadelphia and a return to *My Fair Lady*. Several of the cast members, including Stanley and Hanya Holm ask "How did it go?" Julie also asks, and I still don't know what to say. I wish I had never mentioned the damn audition, and I'm relieved to resume the nightly routine.

I love doing the show. I watch and learn so much about the craft of theater. It's important to my development as an artist, and to my understanding of the values and commitment necessary in making art. It's not easy. It's about high standards, questioning yourself and others, about demanding answers. It's about courage and a sometimes defiant attitude. It ain't for the timid or faint-hearted. And its about craft, the conjuring of make-believe characters with stories to tell. The difficult skills of the violinist are visible, the difficult skills of the actor more ephemeral and transitory.

My Fair Lady opens on March 15, 1956, at the Mark Hellinger Theater on Broadway. Alan Lerner remembers that the opening scene was met with some restraint by the audience. Moss Hart fears the show is just an 'out-of-town' success. Fritz Loewe is sure it will be the biggest hit that had ever come to Broadway. Fritz was right.

The company settles into a comfortable weekly pattern-five evening performances, two matinees. Backstage is usually crowded with celebrities - Marlene Dietrich, Frank Sinatra, Cary Grant, Elizabeth Taylor (God she's beautiful), Katherine Hepburn, Spencer Tracey and others - come to see the show and congratulate the authors and cast.

And an elegant cast party in the lobby of the theater. Teddy Wilson playing the piano, and Fritz - ever the talented composer, never the classy gentleman - telling Julie's visiting mother, "What your daughter needs, Mrs. Andrews, is a good fuck." And Mom replying, "I wouldn't be surprised, Mr. Loewe, I wouldn't be surprised."

I have to play one of Higgin's house servants, standing in for the regular actor who is ill. Rex is getting bored with the nightly routine. He sees that I'm standing in and begins to improvise. "See here," he says, "Bring me a cigar." That dialogue isn't in the scene. I'm not sure what to do, so I do nothing. "Please." He says again, "Bring me a cigar." There's a humidor on the mantle. I bring it down to Rex, offering a cigar. He gives me an astonished look. "What's this?" he says, still improvising. I'm standing there, holding the humidor, looking dumb. "You asked for a cigar, Sir." I say. "No, No" says Rex, "You know I never smoke!" He's a devil when he's bored. I start to laugh, but I know what Rex thinks of actors who break up, and I stifle the urge. Finally the scene is over and we exit. Rex passes me, winks and makes a cluck-cluck sound. Throughout the run of the show he continues to find ways to amuse himself.

The complete cast recording of *My Fair Lady* occurs just days after the opening night. It's recognized as a truly valuable document of a historic moment in American theater. It also becomes a best-seller, allowing CBS to re-coup it's investment in the stage production.

Thinking now about Martin William's reconstructed recordings of musicals for the Smithsonian Collection of Recordings, I realized it was a good effort, but not completely successful. While Martin had to work with fragments of recorded sound, I felt the need for documentation of the original, historic works of music theater - a re-creation for our own time.

TWELVE

The Bicentennial Folklife Festival
Part 1

The two hundredth anniversary of the adoption of the Declaration of Independence was officially celebrated on July 4th, 1976, but plans for a national celebration of America's two hundredth birthday actually began with the appointment of a Bicentennial Commission in 1969. News of the Commission's establishment was overshadowed by Neil Armstrong's and Edwin 'Buzz' Aldrin's landing on the moon. "One small step for man, one giant leap for mankind" easily became the quote of the year.

Also in 1969, President Richard M. Nixon was inaugurated, average annual income was $8,550 and a gallon of gasoline cost 35 cents. In a different sort of celebration, 350,000 came to enjoy the music at Woodstock, New York. Although different in character, demonstrations were also popular, as 250,000 marched on Washington in protest of the Vietnam War.

John Warner, former Assistant secretary of the Navy and future senator from Virginia was named chairman of the Commission in 1974. His assignment was to coordinate the many national Bicentennial celebrations, all of them attempting to find meaning and significance in the occasion. I believed the folklife festival, with its demonstrations of cultural plurality and diversity, would stand out.

In *Celebrating the Bicentennial,* a comprehensive article in the *Museum Journal,* author Victor J. Danilov reported, "The most extensive Bicentennial program is being offered by the Smithsonian Institution in Washington, D.C. With the overall theme of *The American Experience*, it includes twenty-three separate projects involving fifteen bureaus or divisions of the federally operated museum. The Smithsonian's program will be highlighted by the opening of a new building for the National Air and Space Museum. The National Museum of History and Technology will open *We The People*, a major exhibition which takes a reflective look at the American people, and will be followed by *A Nation of Nations*, telling the story of America's evolution from many nations of the world. *Ecology 200-Our Changing Land* will be launched in 1975 by the National Museum of Natural History. The National Portrait Gallery is represented by three major exhibits. The National Collection of Fine Arts, the Renwick Gallery, and the Freer Gallery will add to the Smithsonian presentations. The Smithsonian's newest museum, the Hirshhorn Museum and Sculpture Garden, will open a Bicentennial exhibition titled *The World's Artists and America*: *Immigrants and Refugees.*

136

Among the other activities scheduled by the Smithsonian are traveling exhibits, scholarly research and publications, (including a proposed *Encyclopedia of the American Indian*) and a *Festival of American Folklife*. The festival, presented jointly with the National Park Service for twelve weeks during the summer of 1976, will involve 4500 participants in a series of musical programs, craft demonstrations, storytelling sessions and ethnic food fairs."

Danilov continues with word of Williamsburg, Virginia's day-to-day interpretation of the Virginia colony's history 200 years ago, Old Sturbridge Village's Bicentennial revue called *This Nation, Under God,* The Henry Ford Museum's *Industrial Heritage U.S.A., New York in the New Republic*, by the New York Historical Society, *Leading America into the Twentieth Century*, by the Chicago Historical Society, *The American Farm*, by the California Historical Society, an American Bicentennial Wing and *George Washington, Icon for America*, at the Metropolitan Museum of Art in New York, a celebration of Father Francisco Garce's exploration of the Colorado River, *Paul Revere's Boston, 1735-1818*, at the Boston Museum of Fine Arts, *Birth of a Nation*, at the Huntington Library, Art Gallery and Botanical Gardens, and numerous other exhibits and celebrations. In addition, the number of souvenir sheets, cigarette lighters, spoons, stamps, cups and saucers, Christmas ornaments, beers and whiskeys, hunting knives, playing cards, calendars, pop bottles, buttons and newly minted coins and medals seemed endless.

Danilov concludes "Whether it is because of the economy, the Vietnam war, the energy crisis, the Watergate malaise, or the fumbling of the federal Bicentennial program, the

137

American government, industry and people are not giving wholehearted support to the observance."

Charles Blitzer, now assistant secretary for Art and History, evaluated the Smithsonian proposals and allocated the funds. Two proposals came from the Division of Performing Arts- one proposed the establishment of a jazz program, the other offered plans for the 12 week Bicentennial Folklife Festival.

The quality of the other proposals varied, from the opening of a new National Air and Space Museum to an exhibition of historic coverlets. Other proposals included a recycling of 1876 exhibition items at the Arts and Industries Building, the minting of a new one dollar coin, the exhibition of a Liberty Bell replica made of turkey red wheat and straw, fireworks displays, the publication of an Encyclopedia of the American Indian, and many more.

My plan for a 12-week Bicentennial festival called for presentations that changed each week. Beginning in 1974, yearly festivals would act as rehearsals for the '76 event. Part of our plan included tours of foreign cultural groups to various ethnic festival sites across the U. S. The touring program made the Festival proposal stand out as the Smithsonian's only national outreach effort.

There were no models for a twelve-week festival, little experience to study and few experts to turn to for advice. It had to be a plan imaginative enough to capture attention and maintain that attention from week to week. It had to show a grasp of logistical needs, to project a realistic organizational structure and attract trained and experienced staff. The plan also had to anticipate the cost and have a realistic understanding of the funding sources. Ralph said the plan 'overwhelmed' him.

I divided the Festival presentation into five major elements.

The Old Ways in the New World program was originally Ralph's idea. It was an effort to link traditions from the old world to those of flourishing American ethnic communities. The plan called for coordinated field research in the U. S. and abroad. I added the element of tours-taking foreign participants back to American ethnic communities. Eventually Shirley Cherkasky was named program coordinator for Washington programs and Pat Gebhard and Cynthia Hightower managed the tours.

The Working Americans program presented the culture of people at their work and was first proposed by Archie Green, a San Francisco shipwright, carpenter and folklorist. Green earned his PhD. at the University of Pennsylvania, specializing in occupational folklore. In order to move Working Americans from an idea to a reality, we needed the help and support of the labor movement. I met with Walter Davis, director of education for the AFL/CIO and secured their sponsorship. The program was supported by AFL/CIO President George Meany, a plumber by trade. Shirley Askew was named program coordinator.

The Native Americans program was an outgrowth of several yearly presentations of American Indian culture. We chose the title 'Native Americans' in response to objections by Native groups to the term 'Indian.' Grants from the Bureau of Indian Affairs (BIA) in the Department of the Interior (DoI) aided early planning. Some Native American groups objected to BIA involvement, based on a perceived history of patronizing condescension. We formed a Native American Advisory Group to address the objections and to guide program development. Lucille Dawson was named program coordinator.

The Regional America program grew from the featured state presentations of previous Festivals. Folklorist Henry Glassie originally introduced the idea, drawing on his study of cultural geography and regional vernacular architecture. The concept of American Regionalism had been discussed by cultural historians, geographers and folklorist for years, but always ran into complicating factors and languished. We needed a program that spanned the country, the stakes were high and I thought we should make a try. For some months we floundered. I asked Mack McCormick to examine the idea and he contributed some innovative strategies. The Regional America program continued to evolve through several years of research led by Bess Hawes. Barbara La Pan Rahm was named program coordinator.

The African Diaspora program began in 1973. Originally, an advisory group met to develop a comprehensive statement on the dispersal of black culture in America. Then came research into the survival and flourishing of black cultures in Africa, the Caribbean and America. This research led to the formation of the African Diaspora program. Bernice Johnson Reagon was the driving force of the program, aided by James Early and others. Rosie Lee H. Hooks was named Program Coordinator.

Later on, modest programs in Children's Folklore and Family Folklore were added to the Festival program. The children's program was led by Kate Rinzler; the Family Program by Steve Zeitlin, Sandra Gross and Holly Cutting-Baker.

The Bicentennial Festival plan was a bold concept. Each element had its own character, and much work was required to realize the separate visions. Each element also required different organizational approaches. I wanted trained folklorists in each unit, and that meant recruiting scholars, researchers, teachers and graduate students from museums, colleges and universities. I sought experienced designers, administrators, travel personnel and technical support staff for each unit. With help from Smithsonian personnel, procurement and supply offices, systems for obtaining equipment, professional services and supplies had to be developed.

We taped a brown wrapping paper planning chart to our conference room wall to track assignments and progress. At the top of this planning chart was a space labeled 'fund raising' Discussions with folklife and administrative staff about money needs were heated, and often naïve. I was troubled by the consistent use of passive language, as in, 'funds must be found.' I worked to change the group mindset from passive to active, to identify 'who must find the funds.' These efforts were seldom successful.

The Smithsonian administration reviewed and approved our plan with a major caveat: a substantial part of the needed money must come from non-Smithsonian sources.

Why this stipulation? I don't know the answer. Perhaps it was to challenge my ability, my commitment, my determination. Perhaps it was a desire to gain a large-scale, highly visible program at little cost or risk. Maybe it was a lack of institutional belief in the core folk culture program. Learning the real answer wouldn't have made any difference.

I was happy that James Morris III – now known as 'Jim'- worked on the festivals. It was a great way for him to spend his summers and it was my gift to him.

Meanwhile we had performances to produce, and recordings to issue.

THIRTEEN

Interim

Smithsonian Magazine published its first issue in 1970 and enrolled some 635,000 national member/subscribers - dubbed Smithsonian Associates – in its first year. We placed ads for *Classic Jazz* in the magazine, and sent solicitations by mail to Smithsonian Associates. Income from these early marketing efforts brought in $400,000.

By 1977 *Smithsonian Magazine* had enrolled some 1,300,000 Associate members, and we began regular marketing efforts for all the Smithsonian Collection of Recordings. The initial direct mail marketing campaigns drew approximately 39,000 responses and generated some $780,000 in sales income. Additional mailings continued for months until, in 1979, *Classic Jazz* was awarded a Gold Record, indicating sales of $1 million dollars. Later, *Classic Jazz* was awarded a Platinum Record, indicating one million records sold. After several years *Classic Jazz* became an "evergreen," attaining triple-platinum status, and other items from the Smithsonian Collection of Recordings continued strong sales.

In truth, I was surprised by this response. I did not know what to expect, but years of reading publication news, scouring library shelves and book and record stores told me that there were serious gaps in information about jazz and other areas of American culture. I did not know how recordings produced by the Division of Performing Arts would be received, but I had a hunch. So the enthusiastic reception by critics, academics, the press and the public at large made me very happy. I was surprised that a direct mail marketing effort would produce such unprecedented results, and I was somewhat disappointed that the response from the Smithsonian administration dealt mainly with the money we were making rather than our contribution to knowledge.

The exception was Julian Ewell, a caring and supportive boss, and he was enthused by our success.

I remember a quote from Henry Ford. "Money doesn't change men, it only unmasks them." And true to form, our commercial success unmasked a passion for money.

We were the bureau credited with turning the Smithsonian into a 'living museum,' Now, in a matter of weeks, we were making money! The administration wanted all income sent to the general treasury. I fought for a better deal, an agreement whereby a reasonable percentage of sales income would go to new product and program development. I won the first round, but it was a temporary victory.

As part of new product and program development, I used some of the income from *Classic Jazz* to support under-funded projects of the Division of Musical Instruments. Their production of Philippe Rameau's opera ballet, *La Naissance d'Osiris*, with reconstructed dances by dance historian Shirley Wynne, added to a growing international interest in early music and dance. Wynne also choreographed *There's a Good Time Coming,* an evening of 19th Century American music and ballroom dancing, staged in the Renwick Gallery's Grand Salon. I was impressed with Wynne's scholarship and theatricality and with Jim Weaver's musical leadership and entrepreneurial flare.

We continued to develop programs in jazz, folk music and dance. With a talented young pianist named Rob Fisher we developed a musical theater presentational style - no sets, few props and visible accompaniment – a style that presaged New York City's highly successful *Encore* series.

We demonstrated how performances could be successful interpretive tools for museums, colleges and universities and we showed how museums, with their collections of art and artifacts, were ideal environments for the preservation and study of performance practices. The subject of performance practices was well known to early music scholars, but it was not of common interest to musical historians of the 20th century. Broadway shows were orchestrated by people like Leo Arnaud, Willard Robison and particularly Hans Spialek, who scored some twenty musicals in the 1930's and '40's. The recent discovery of manuscripts stored in a New Jersey warehouse brought to life many of Spialek's orchestrations, and they differ in style and instrumentation from the scores available from commercial rental libraries. I intended to join with curators in the Museum of American History to recover and restore the work of Spialek and others, and to use these

145

original orchestrations in our recordings. We would then be introducing a new application of performance practices research.

I was enthusiastic about our mixture of classical, popular and folk culture programs, and about the recordings we were producing. I was also pleased that the mixture led to a lively debate in the press and national arts community.

My personal interest was in 20th century American popular songs and musical theater. Martin's focus was jazz and he was also responsible for the Oxford University Press publication of Michael Barrier's *Hollywood Cartoons: American Animation in its Golden Age*. Martin also wrote a book about the early films of D. W. Griffith and co-edited *A Smithsonian Book of Comic-Book Comics*. These publications were praised by critics, and they made money. And at the same time, the National Endowment for the Arts gave the Division of Performing Arts a grant to administer a Jazz oral history project. Martin was to supervise, and we hired J. R. Taylor, a young scholar with broad interest in cultural affairs, to conduct the interviews. The transcribed interviews brought a new source to the study of jazz history.

Contentious opinions are common in academia, so I was not surprised by occasional criticism that our folk culture programs shied away from subjects like folk medicine and religion. So-called 'folk medicine' often included claims and stories of miraculous healing that had plagued established medicine for centuries. 'Folk religion' included faith healing, fetishes, voodoo, magic and witchcraft - elements of traditional culture that cast an ominous shadow on innocent genres like folk songs and folk tales. I didn't ignore the

146

criticism, and thought these subjects should be interesting challenges for the future.

Cultural views of a different sort underscored my relationship with Ralph Rinzler. On one occasion Ralph had said "I find jazz a hostile, disturbing kind of music." On other occasions he disparaged popular culture genres like operetta, musical theater, popular songs and television comedy but displayed a refined taste in traditional folk music. Our opinions differed substantially but I thought our differences were stimulating.

As time passed Ralph grew unhappy with his role in our operations, and with my leadership. He made his complaints known during the annual meeting of the American Folklore Society (AFS). As a result, two AFS members, Roger Abrahams and Robert Byington, came to Washington and met with Julian Euell, requesting autonomy for Ralph. Julian responded that he was content with my leadership and would not consider a change in assignments. For my part, I was unhappy with Ralph, and with Abrahams and Byington. I thought their actions cast unjustified criticism on my efforts to build the Folklife Festival into a continuing Smithsonian program. Their criticisms were not explicit or substantive, and I resented the fact that they excluded me from their discussions with Euell. Ralph's actions in instigating this meeting could be seen as insubordinate and I could have fired him. Instead, I heeded Julian's advice and let the matter pass. My decision was a mistake.

Our differences were symptomatic of a wider debate about American culture. Musicologist Richard Middleton, coordinating editor of the journal, *Popular Music*, reported,

"The terminology of historical musicology is slanted by the needs of classical music and may overlook areas such as rhythm, pitch, nuance and gradation, and timbre. Some musicologists act as though popular music did not exist."

Did not exist? I agreed with Middleton, and thought the cited musicologists were out of touch with an America awash in popular culture. I also believed that popular music, so primal, so involved with feelings, was a true reflection of contemporary American society and could not be ignored in programming created by museums and cultural centers. It made me happy that my years of eclectic musical involvement and theatrical experiences made it possible for me the make artistic contributions.

I enjoyed the different opinions and encouraged the debates. It was fun, and stimulating, and I never thought the give and take revealed animosity by any of the parties. I may have been distracted by the birth of a second son – Joseph Adam Morris, born January 25, 1972. We called him Adam, and he was the most appealing baby I had ever known. His laughter came easily, his affection was distributed to one and all, and I was certain he displayed signs of a keen intelligence.

FOURTEEN

The Bicentennial Folklife Festival
Part II

So the time came when it was necessary to answer the question, "Who must find the funds?" And the obvious answer came, loud and clear. *I'm the who - the who who must find the funds.* There wasn't anyone else, and I was very aware that a substantial part of Festival costs must come from non-Smithsonian sources.

In 1974 I learned that the Office of Management and Budget had included funds for a Bicentennial Folklife Festival in the Smithsonian's annual Federal Appropriation. The Division of Performing Arts was to receive multi-year funding for Festival planning and production. But the Smithsonian request had been far less than my cost projections for a 12-week 1976 Festival. While I had planned on some money coming from grants and contracts I hoped to negotiate, there was still a two million dollar shortfall. To give us an adequate budget, this amount must now be raised from corporations or private donors.

I needed help. I interviewed several professional fund raisers, and finally chose Walker Williams, a bright, personable young man with contacts in philanthropic foundations and in the corporate world. Walker quickly grasped the Festival's appeal and he was free of the cant and hypocrisy that seemed to infect other fund raisers. He advised that I should be the Smithsonian's point person, reasoning that a donor would want to know the individual responsible for the wise use of their money.

The 1974 Folklife Festival was, in many ways, a rehearsal for the 12-week Bicentennial event. To provide enough physical space, we redesigned the site and moved to an area near the Lincoln Memorial and the Reflecting Pool.

The featured state was Mississippi. Sweden, Norway, Finland, Tunisia and Greece inaugurated the Old Ways in the New World program. The African Diaspora program included participants from Ghana, Trinidad, Tobago and Nigeria, plus American musicians and crafts people from Mississippi. The Working Americans program highlighted communication workers, and was presented in cooperation with the new George Meany Center for Labor Studies.

Looking forward to increased foreign participation, I relied on the Smithsonian Office of International and Environmental Programs (OIEP) for advice and guidance. OIEP was originally established to administer foreign currency grants, and was headed by Wymberley Coerr, former U. S. Ambassador to Uruguay and Ecuador. Veteran Foreign Service professionals Richard Conroy and Alan Lester were detailed by the Department of State to assist us in diplomatic negotiations and visa administration.

Ralph was fluent in French, and he was a skillful negotiator. He made the Old Ways program his priority, identifying ethnic participants and field researchers. Shirley Cherkasky, as program coordinator, added her substantial administrative and planning skills.

Walker Williams and I assembled a modest fund raising slide show. Our first presentations were to the Ford Foundation and the Rockefeller Foundation - the largest philanthropic donors to cultural programs. Both Foundations turned us down.

Appeals to other foundations netted no results. None of the foundations were clear about their reasons for refusing our appeal. Some stated that we did not 'fall within their established guidelines.' Others were confused by competing Smithsonian requests. We turned instead to the business world.

Using the New York City offices of *Smithsonian Magazine*, we made dozens of corporate presentations, often as many as three each day. Walker did a good job in identifying decision makers. The presentations were well attended and people were pleasant, but we discovered no prospects.. An association with the Smithsonian, and a Bicentennial promotional opportunity didn't light any fires.

I was not going to be deterred, and we persisted. At times I was discouraged by the turn-downs, but I believed in the Festival and its celebration of the common man. I also believed that America's birthday, and the American experience, was a good and worthy reason for celebration.

151

Walker kept my spirits up. Julian Euell added regular support and inspiration, and we pushed ahead.

We talked to insurance companies, banks, auto manufacturers, clothing manufacturers, breweries, steel and aluminum producers, drug companies, railroad operators, restaurant chains, real estate developers, building contractors, recreational groups, marketing firms, communication corporations, hotel chains, engineering firms, electronic equipment makers, energy conglomerates, plastics manufacturers, medical suppliers, and others. Everyone was polite. Many were interested in the Bicentennial, but not ready to commit money. On a long holiday Easter weekend I became depressed. My confidence was slipping. Then we had the first positive response.

A vice president at General Foods Corporation liked folk music, and he attended a presentation. At home, his children expressed their enthusiasm for the idea. General Foods had a large number of products to promote, including coffee, baking supplies, cereals, frozen foods —and Jello. I went to their corporate officers in White Plains, N. Y. to present the Festival idea.

A few days later they called, pledging a one million dollar gift.

The General Foods gift was followed by American Airlines. One of their executives saw a business opportunity in our extensive travel budget. The president of the corporation, a pound-the-table type, called. In return for sponsorship, he wanted all the airline travel channeled through American Airlines. I said I could not do that. He hung up, and I thought that was the end of it. The following day an American representative called. They agreed to my conditions, and pledged another million dollars.

With our two, million-dollar donors in hand, I turned to other sources. I met with numerous government bureaus and non-profit groups. I thought that many of these agencies would want a presence in the Bicentennial celebration. I also believed that with some creative thought, we could find ways for their participation within the broad themes of the festival program. And we had the national Mall. We had the prestigious platform, and the established visibility. And we had the support of Peter Fannon, Bicentennial program coordinator for the Office of Management and Budget. Peter liked the festival idea, especially the touring of foreign cultural groups to American ethnic communities. His opinion carried substantial weight.

**Dancers, Old Ways in the New World program,
Festival of American Folklife**

By 1976, when the summer Festival opened, more than seventeen bureaus, corporations and non-profit organizations had become principal sponsors. They comprised a disparate group of funding sources with different expectations and motives. They required almost constant attention, but in the end their contributions were significant - and our total operating budget grew to more than 7 million dollars

Our1974/75 concert season continued, with a full slate of fall, winter and spring performance activities. Jazz Heritage concerts included Bill Evans, Roy Eldridge, Marian McPartland, Dizzy Gillespie, Randy Weston, The Heath Brothers, Teddy Wilson, Hank Jones, and John Lewis. Popular song programs included Margaret Whiting, John Raitt, Bobby Short, Jimmy Witherspoon, Mabel Mercer and the Mills Brothers.The Division of Musical Instruments concerts featured Concentus Musicus Wein, Jan De Gaetani, Gustave Leonhardt – and with the Kennedy Center for the Performing Arts – a Franz Joseph Haydn Festival. Theater and dance programs included the National Shadow Theater of Malaysia, the Heen Baba Dance Ensemble of Ceylon, the Noh/Kyogen National Theater of Japan, the Burmese National Theater and the Lhamo Folk Opera of Tibet. We also presented a full season of Discovery Theater productions. We elected to spin-off sponsorship of the American College Theater Festival to the Kennedy Center for the Performing Arts.

In addition to the live programs, we produced 12 new record albums of Baroque, jazz and musical theater. The 1975 Folklife Festival was another Bicentennial rehearsal. Participants included Native Americans from the Iroquois Confederacy and regional American communities from the Northern Plains and the California heartland. An improved Working American's program showcased transportation with railroad workers, aircraft employees, and truckers. Participants in Old Ways in the New World came from Germany, Italy, Lebanon, Japan and Mexico. African Diaspora participants came from Jamaica, Haiti, and Ghana, and there were several children's groups. Fund raising success allowed us to recruit an exceptionally able and dedicated staff. Time has passed - I could never remember them all - but I do remember:

Richard (Dick) Lusher was my deputy, a thoughtful, creative administrator, and with the assistance of Ken Dresser, Dick designed the layout of the Festival. He also supervised the erection and installation of exhibit buildings, tents structures, communications systems and public accommodations.

Chris Atkins, Kim Baer, Saul Baran, Bruce Buckley, Harold Closter, Susan Cox, Norma Graus, Barrick Groom, Cynthia Hightower, Ruth Jordan, Naomi Kaitz, Alan Lester, Manuel Melendez, Saucie Melnicove, Jim Moon, Diana Parker, Marce Pollan, Robert Porter, Gail Obenreder, Mary Stewart and Abby Watkins and others served on the Division of Performing Arts staff.

Ralph Rinzler remained the festival director. Bob Byington, Lucille Dawson, Roland Freeman, Archie Green, Bess Lomax Hawes, Susan Kalcik, Tom Kavanagh, Amy Kotkin, Worth Long, Bob McCarl, Mack McCormick, Bill McNeil, Ken Periman, David Plowden, Frank Proschan, Jack Santino, Mike Seeger, Peter Seitel, Barre Toelkin, William Wiggins, Tom Vennum and others served on the festival staff.

Betty Beuck, Eva Elliot, Ken Dresser, Brock Holmes, Jennifer Hope, B. C. May, Ernestine Potter, Peter Reiniger,

Sally Roffman, Suzanne Roschwalb, Janet Stratton and others served on the administrative, production and public information staff, In the spring, we moved our offices to several rented trailers on the Mall.

The National Mall is often seen as an emblem- an icon. It has been called "the Axis of the Nation, Our American Symbol, Our Front Yard and Our Democratic Stage." And across the street from the Mall is the National Archives, home of the original Declaration of Independence and the Constitution of the United States.

The National Mall and Memorial Parks – their official designations – were established in 1965 to commemorate presidential legacies, to honor the courage and sacrifice of war veterans and to celebrate the United States commitment to freedom and equality. The area includes the Capitol and the Lincoln Memorial, the east and west wing of the National Gallery of Art and Sculpture Garden, The National Museum of Natural History, the National Museum of American History, the U. S. Grant Memorial, and the National Botanic Gardens, the Arts and Industry Building, the original Smithsonian Building and the Freer Gallery of Art. Relative newcomers to the Mall are the National Museum of the American Indian, the National Air and Space Museum, and the Hirshhorn Museum and Sculpture Garden.

The Mall is also home to several other national icons, including the Washington Monument, the Thomas Jefferson Memorial, the Franklyn Delano Roosevelt Memorial, the Korean War Veterans Memorial, the Vietnam Veterans Memorial and later, the World War II Memorial.

This was our theater, the site where we to produce the Mall's largest and most complex cultural event.

Our master plan called for some 5,000 artists from the United States and 35 foreign countries to participate in festival programs. There would be a complete change of participants every seven days for 12 weeks – virtually a new festival program each week. Participants were selected by a team of researchers who determined what activity they would bring to the festival, what celebrations or crafts or skills they would demonstrate, what music or dance or type of theater they would perform, what food or ritual they would share. Selected participants were then contacted by Performing Arts staff to determine special personal and dietary needs, supplies and material requirements and to make travel and housing arrangements. After their appearance on the Mall, many foreign participants would join local, ethnic and community celebrations across the U.S.

The Bicentennial Folklife Festival commenced on June 16th, 1976, on the National Mall and adjacent to the large reflecting pool. Bicentennial Coordinator John Warner, Secretary Ripley and other notable make welcoming speeches, and Ripley said, "What we have hoped-and we have seen to come to pass in many places-is that our Festival would illuminate the many roads to better understanding of our varied cultures, that our visitors would return home to create their own celebrations out of their own cultural resources in their own local museums and schools. In the summer of the Bicentennial, you may find at our Festival not only a shared delight in the beauty of craft, dance and music, but a deeper commitment to the creative energies which everywhere inform the human spirit."

There was a 48-page souvenir program book, with weekly supplements containing up-to-date lists of participants and daily events and performance schedules, edited by Bess Lomax Hawes and Susanne Roschwalb. The colorful cover design was a scenic tapestry depicting the entire Festival and hand stitched by Mrs. Ethel Wright Mohamed of Belzoni, Mississippi.

Folklife Festival Tapestry,
created by Ethel Wright Mohamed, 1976

Writing in *Red Book Magazine*, famed anthropologist Margaret Mead added, "While we are celebrating the different kinds of people who are Americans and the different things Americans have done with song and dance and food, in work-ways and play-ways, we are celebrating the diversity of people everywhere."

Alan Lomax, co-founder of the Archive of American Folk Song at the Library of Congress wrote, "The Festival of

American Folklife makes a further step forward for our folk artists. Here the fiddlers, the blues guitarist, the blanket weavers, the cooks, the Mariachi musicians and the telephone linemen—brought from all over the United States and set down in the midst of the most powerful national symbols-can step out on the stage and receive the attention they deserve."

George Meany, president of the AFL-CIO wrote, "One hundred years ago, when America celebrated its centennial, the theme was the industrial revolution – the machines that ran the country, not the people who built it. This time it is going to be different. It's not the machines that make America great. It is her people – the workers who build, clothe, feed, communicate, entertain and transport us. The AFL-CIO, the largest trade union in the world, is proud to participate in the 1976 Festival of American Folklife."

Ralph Rinzler, festival director, wrote, "Festivals strengthen a people's sense of community by ritualizing common experience. State festivals and folklore programs have been established in most of the states featured in past Festivals. As a result of the Festival, the National Endowment for the Arts has established two granting programs in folk culture and Congress has passed legislation establishing a National Folklife Center at the Library of Congress."

As Festival producer, my program article remembered historian Constance Rourke, who pioneered the study of American culture and reminded us of "the common 1930's belief that Americans had no aesthetic tradition of their own, and that the country had never produced a culture in which the arts could flourish." Rourke observed that we, as a nation, "had accepted this notion and developed the habit of importing our art." I also criticized "a national cultural policy, expressed in arts education formulae and government and foundation grants, that was designed to develop a nation of consumers." I also decried "government funding for the arts that has helped arts organization survive if they will not be offensive, will shun rude sounds and startling unconventional images, and avoid challenging and provocative subjects-when one of arts key functions is to challenge and provoke."

The Bicentennial Folklife Festival received enthusiastic response from the press, from sponsors and funding sources, and from institutional leaders. I particularly enjoyed the reactions away from the Mall and away from Washington., in communities across the country. Many American communities invited Festival participants to visit their towns and cities. In these locales, ethnic community groups, bicentennial committees, arts councils, parks and recreational departments, museums and colleges and universities joined with local and regional businesses to organize celebrations of their own, and the centerpiece of these celebrations came from the Festival of American Folklife.

Throughout the entire 12 weeks of Festival presentations, there were no public disturbances, no untoward behavior. And to the surprise of many, we were able to sustain public interest and involvement throughout the entire period.

African Diaspora Processional, Folklife Festival, 1976

Public dancing, Folklife Festival, 1976

I began each day by walking through the various program areas, talking with staff and participants, seeing demonstrations and listening to performances. At one time or

161

another I heard a Romanian folk orchestra, a Delta blues band, Swedish folk fiddlers, unaccompanied American ballad singers, a German marching band, Galician bagpipers, a Mariachi band, a night-life scene from Zaire and Surinam, a union workers song swap, Alpine yodelers, Macedonian instrumentalists and singers, Italian bagpipers, singers from Nova Scotia and more. I had a wonderful time!

At various times we had interesting and distinguished visitors to the Festival. Vice President Rockefeller visited on several occasions, riding over the grounds in a golf cart.. Members of Congress were a common sight at concerts and craft demonstrations, as were members of the cabinet. The General Foods Corporation invited their Board of Directors and friends to a reception on the Mall. American Airlines corporate executives toured the grounds in golf carts. King Juan Carlos and Queen Sophia of Spain attended, and Queen Elizabeth II of Great Brittan paid us a visit I was selected, along with Secretary Ripley, to be presented to Her Majesty, and I received coaching in proper deportment by Embassy staff.

Jill Lepore, a Harvard historian says, "The American Revolution is everyone's favorite event. When in doubt, in American politics - left right or center - deploy the Founding Fathers. Predictably, the occasion of a Bicentennial was used by anti-war groups to justify their opposition to the nation's involvement in Viet Nam."

In her recent book, *The Whites of their Eyes; the Tea Party Revolution and the Battle Over American History,* Lepore writes about the tension between critical history and popular memory, and she cites the difference between American

162

history in the eyes of historians and the history that society chooses to remember.

The popularity of the Bicentennial Folklife Festival celebrated American culture as remembered by a majority. Writing in the *New York Review of Books*, Brown University Historian Emeritus Gordon S. Wood says "this sort of collective memory is essential for any society" and he points to English historian Davis Lowenthal who labels this collective memory 'heritage.'

Back in the trailer that served as my on-the-Mall office I would marvel once again at the powerful ways music evoked emotions as it underscored scenes of war, flooding, earthquakes and fire. I thought about the marriage of words and music heard at various Festival sites, the songs of people at work, at play, in devotions and in love.

I had long since learned that the Smithsonian Institution, by its nature, was a peculiar organization. It was the world's largest museum complex with nine museums in Washington and New York City, numerous research centers, archives, libraries, gardens and various complex data bases. It was an academic, educational establishment whose structure is similar to a university and a research facility, with separate fields of interests fiercely competing for resources and priorities. Three quarters of the institution is funded by the Federal Government-one quarter by private funds, endowments and earned business income. Those who study organizational functioning have described it as a five-dimensional model (bureaucratic, collegial, political, anarchical, cybernetic.) Managing such an organization has been described as similar to herding cats.

The Division of Performing Arts was among the newest Smithsonian organizations. Early programs were created as a response to Secretary Ripley's desire to bring life and vitality to the Mall and to the museums. Beginning with the Folklife Festival we moved that idea past animation to a series of programs that addressed the American aesthetic experience, and to subjects that had, sadly, been overlooked or ignored by museums and academia. A museum's desire to collect was undeniably important, but for all the iconic significance of a mass produced instrument belonging to Louis Armstrong, I was less interested in collecting Louis' horn than in understanding the music Louis made with it.

From the outset we saw performances as more than entertainment. We saw the research of repertory and environment resulting in increased understanding of historic repertory and performance practices. We saw the publication of recordings, musical scores and monographs as important academic publications. And we saw the response of educational organizations, museums, conservatories and the public as verification of our vision. Our programs in jazz, blues, baroque and classical music, folk culture and American popular culture, theater and popular music, modern dance and African-American culture, began to move the Smithsonian in new and exciting directions.

The Folklife Festival was the signature program of the Smithsonian's Division of Performing Arts. It demonstrated our ability to research, produce, document and present creative elements of American and world cultures. With careful nurturing, the Festival had accumulated friends and supporters in many areas – academic, popular, political,

164

financial and institutional. Following the great popular success of the Bicentennial Festival I believed the Festival would help us generate public support and money for scholarship and production in other less well known – less popular areas.

FIFTEEN

Ralph Rinzler

For ten years, Ralph and I worked together. It's fair to say that we were close in our philosophy, in our opinions and in our goals. In the early years, when our staff was small and everyone joined in all the tasks of planning and producing the Folklife Festival, we shared correspondence, phone calls, personal meetings–all manner of communication about Festival matters.

It was quite common for Ralph to call me from some location in the field, call from a phone booth or a bar or a private home - at any hour of the day or night – to share his enthusiasm for a recent discovery or interview. We were both excited by our work, and shared our excitement at new discoveries. An office visitor, bringing new and important information about the folk culture world, would prompt a visit from Ralph to my office to share that information. Ralph often responded to significant happenings with a personal note, saying on many occasions, "...how much I value our working relationship." Or ..."it's gratifying to have this success and it wouldn't have happened without you." I never questioned the sincerity of these reactions, and I cherished them.

When my mother was confined to a nursing home after a fall, Ralph brought her flowers and a tape recorder with an assortment of music to hear. When my wife and I mourned the loss of a new-born child, he provided recorded music for the memorial service. And there were the frequently exchanged gifts of music or books to share.

It is in this context that I was surprised by Ralph's several resignations. He wrote a letter of resignation in reaction to the shooting of Kent State University students. He wrote again saying he wished to pursue publishing opportunities and again when I committed the Division of Performing Arts to a large Bicentennial Festival. On each of these occasions I urged him to reconsider. And he did.

Ralph was an excellent field researcher. In the mold of Alan Lomax, he could enter a community and easily ingratiate himself. He had an excellent eye for crafts. He used his talents as a guitar and mandolin player to establish an empathetic bond with local musicians. In the process of documenting his research he became a good photographer and an adept audio recorder, and he maintained credibility and good relations with academic folklorists.

Then, after a ten year relationship, I saw our comradeship began to disintegrate. I could see it in the withdrawal of shared communications, in absences from the offices, in the missing solidarity. I could also hear it in the changing choice of words and tone, and in new relationships – as when he began to write personal notes and address Secretary Ripley as 'Dillon,' signifying a first-name intimacy that I and others did not presume or duplicate.

I thought carefully about the change in our relationship. I knew that there were occasions when I made decisions that were not to Ralph's liking. I reckoned that these decisions were made for the long-term benefit and health of our organization and our programs and that all these decisions were openly discussed and shared with everyone, including my supervisors. And to my knowledge none of these decisions were arbitrary or capricious.

In time I came to believe that our problems might be traced to our success, and that Ralph began to think of himself as the primary reason for that success. I think he wanted sole ownership of a very popular event, and that desire led him to seek autonomy.

On the several occasions when Ralph directly asked for autonomy, I was surprised, and thought his requests were presumptuous. His requests were denied, first by me, then by Assistant Secretary Euell and others. In his work with subordinates, I thought he played favorites and did not make a wise allocation of resources. Although he contributed creative ideas to the Festival's development, the Festival was, after all, my idea. It had brought credit to me and the organization I headed and I saw no reason to step aside. I was told by Euell and others that their denials of Ralph's requests for autonomy were based on fair assessments, concluding that Ralph did not show management experience or the ability to supervise a complex event. I believe the

169

Smithsonian's treasurer and the chief administrator concurred in the assistant secretary's decision.

Unfortunately, these decisions added to an air of antipathy and did not end what had the appearance of a power struggle. In the often confusing management style of the Smithsonian this antipathy was allowed to fester. This style often expressed itself on the one hand in a disorienting anarchy that resisted a clear chain of command, and on the other hand in a more authoritarian 'castle law' (my castle-my rules).

In the months leading up to the Bicentennial Folklife Festival, the struggles took several forms. At one point, reacting to a rumor, Ripley considered charging me with maladministration for making unfunded financial obligations. This charge was investigated, found to be without merit, and dismissed as hearsay. At another point Assistant Secretary Euell and I were questioned about a missing memorandum addressed to Secretary Ripley. It was said the subject memorandum, complaining that I ignored the priorities of folklorists in the allocation of funds, had been suppressed. Both Euell and I denied any unfair allocation of funds or any suppression of communications. Despite a thorough search, the subject memorandum, with its charges, was never found. In another instance I was criticized for my personal involvement in popular culture recordings of historic American musical theater. This criticism was dismissed with the citation of strongly favorable critical and academic responses to the recordings.

The Bicentennial Folklife Festival ended with a balanced budget, praise from members of Congress, the public and the press, plus kudos for all concerned. *Washingtonian Magazine* recognized both Ralph and me with this citation:

"They built the Smithsonian's Folklife Festival from a quiet affair in 1967 to a 12-week 1976 extravaganza with 5,000 participants, a six million dollar budget and an audience of five million. They have combined a world-wide search for regional folklife – a sort of scholarly detective work – with a lively presentation on the Mall each summer. And in the process they have won respectability for folk art, crafts and traditions, some of which were being forgotten. For creating a popular festival, producing it expertly and giving people a happy educational experience each summer, James Morris and Ralph Rinzler are *Washingtonian's of the Year.*"

Ralph and I attended the Washingtonian-of-the-Year Award dinner. We each made a short acceptance speech - Ralph insisted I speak first - and I thanked him for his contributions to the Festival. He smiled broadly and seemed to enjoy the recognition. So did I.

In the fall and winter of 1976/77 there were intense discussions within Smithsonian management about the future of the Folklife Festival. A committee of Assistant Secretaries recommended that I continue in charge of the Festival. Ralph disagreed, and made a strong personal appeal to Secretary Ripley. The history of bogus charges, non-existent memoranda, and demands for autonomy had created a toxic environment that corrupted healthy deliberations. When discussions began to trade in hyperbole rather than rhetoric, I was appalled. When hyperbole became virulent, I resigned as Festival producer, to work on a wide variety of other cultural projects.

SIXTEEN

A Unique Cultural Resource

To tell the truth, the post-Bicentennial experiences left me mad as hell. I had been asked to bring a calcified institution to life, to conceptualize and nurture change. I had also been asked to build support for change, so I rehearsed it, tested it, critiqued it, fixed it, managed it and built on success.

In a review of the Festival by Smithsonian management it was acknowledged that the Bicentennial Folklife Festival was well planned and managed. It was a huge, complex production that had operated on time, on budget and largely problem free.

Building on success meant using the credibility, the tested formulas and techniques to address areas of need. In addition to enlivenment, it meant addressing 'neglected and misunderstood aspects of our national culture.'

I walked away from the Festival and sought some healing in nostalgia, remembering a time when I was free of administrative pressures and making music was my only concern; a time when my society was a coterie of loyal and caring friends. I remembered the two cold water flats on Manhattan's east side, with the bathtubs in the kitchen and the toilet down the hall, apartments shared with fellow Juilliard students Don Pippin and Martha (Jackie) Frasier. Jackie was a talented soprano, Don a gifted pianist who became the Tony Award winning conductor of Broadway musicals like *Oliver, Mame, A Chorus Line* and many others. I remembered Don's understanding and appreciation of musical theater, an American art form, and Lehman Engel's description of our musical theater as a "seamless construction of songs, dance and dialogue knit together – better than any other theater." I thought about Ernestine Perrie's belief that "the theater was about the search for truth and understanding."

It was a sweet time. Our lives were like a scene from the opera, *La Boheme*, a community of young artists filled with hope and in love with life.

Now, my original Smithsonian assignment isn't finished. Some 'living museum' models are successfully adopted by other museums, others provoke reassessment and change. Music and dance companies from Africa and Asia enliven our ethnological exhibitions.

Collaboration with the Division of Musical Instruments has been a desire, and now it happens. BASF, the international chemical company, gives money for *Music and Dance from the Age of Jefferson*. The gift yields a stage production and a recording; with music and social dance from the period. The key figures are Jim Weaver, dance historian

Shirley Wynn and me. After the Washington performance there's an offer to bring the show to the Cleveland Museum of Art, with dances now created by historian Wendy Heller. It's an interesting show, based on an unusual concept, scholarship and showmanship. Audiences like it, the sponsor likes it and Ripley is pleased with the Cleveland Museum association. The collaboration sparks conversations about the future, perhaps a Smithsonian Chamber Orchestra-a baroque and classical 'big band.' I believe we're moving in the right direction, but I'm concerned about the 'neglected and misunderstood.'

So we re-organize and plan. The recording program, touring performances and the Discovery Theater are grouped into an Office of Education Services. Cynthia Hightower did an outstanding job managing travel and logistics for the ethnic tour program, and staffing advisor Saul Baran recommends Cynthia to head the new operation. Brock Holmes, J. R. Taylor, Bill Bennett, Judy Gumbita, Louise Neu and Jane Sapp are assigned to the group, and Lynn Brice Rooney is hired to develop Discovery Theater programs. Sally Roffman will market our products.

To be sure that Education Services programs and recordings are sensible and comprehensive, we create an advisory committee, chaired by Cynthia. Smithsonian staff members include Taylor, Bennett, Sapp, and Weaver, plus Bernice Reagon, Martin Williams, Cynthia Hoover, Ralph Rinzler, Glenn Ruh and Carl Scheele. Public members include David Hall (Library and Museum of the Performing Arts at Lincoln Center,) Charles Rosen (pianist, critic and author,)

Smithsonian Impresario

Wayne Shirley (Library of Congress) and Horace Boyer (University of Massachusetts scholar.)

We also enlist some advocates. One is Tom T. Hall, country music star and composer of songs for Johnny Cash, George Jones, Loretta Lynn and Wayland Jennings. Another advocate is Sylvia Fine, i.e. Mrs. Danny Kaye. Hall proves to be a person of deep intelligence. Ms Fine, who wrote the multisyllabic doubletalk that characterizes much of Kaye's early success, now produces television documentaries, and she is a passionate and informed musical theater supporter.

James Weaver joins our staff while continuing to work with instruments from the Smithsonian's historic collection – and 'to make them sing again.' I believe this work, which includes the study of performance practices throughout musical history, is very important and deserves strong institutional support.

The Esterhazy Machine, Steven Dann, violin; Kenneth Slowik, baryton; Myron Lutze, cello; nb The barton is an instrament of the viol famly, with six bowed strings and ten sympathetic strings

Jim directs our numerous chamber music programs and participates in other activities. He also conducts a recorded performance of Handel's *Messiah*, using period instruments. With the recording, listeners may experience sounds similar to those heard by an audience in Dublin in 1742, when the composer first conducted it.

With concerts of jazz, the blues, musical theater, popular song and dance, I believe we are indeed promoting knowledge and appreciation of American cultural achievements-the 'neglected and misunderstood.' There's an interesting development, a verification of sorts, when we are approached by the Music Critics Association requesting that we offer

177

workshops on criticism in jazz and popular culture. The workshops generate stimulating discussions, and occasional arguments. The give-and-take educates us all and I hope we will broaden and enrich critical knowledge and vocabulary.

To pay for operations, I rely on income from record sales and ticket sales, plus funds from Smithsonian non-Federal, trust fund sources. In addition, we have a yearly Federal fund appropriation that covers some personnel costs, with a small amount of money for other expenses. Recordings are produced by Education Services; ticketed events - jazz concerts, musical instrument concerts, country music concerts, musical theater and popular song performances, and musical theater - are produced by Peggy Martin, Sharyn Reitz and Cindy Hutchins; Black culture programs are produced by Bernice and her staff, while Bernice, Jim Weaver, Harold Closter, Martin Williams and I provide content expertise.

In addition to recordings, Sally will also manage ticket sales. And Sally also produces *Living Museum*, a film about our programs. The film is popular with Ripley, who screens it at various meetings and conferences as a documentary about his ideas on museum learning.

This is our 'business model.' I use the term sarcastically, because no 'business model' would be worth a glance without some measurement standards. From my point of view, Smithsonian measurements are subjective, biased and useless. But what passes for a business model is operated by a wonderful staff, with great teamwork, great camaraderie. And we have the unstinting support of Julian Euell.

While I'm grateful for any support we receive, I often feel like I'm steering a high-powered vehicle while sitting on an unwieldy and unbalanced three-legged stool. That business model is unwieldy and difficult to manage. I submit a yearly budget, knowing that a budget is a political document and that the availability of funds doesn't conform to a calendar. Commitments to artists must be made months or years in advance and income from sales is volatile and has its own schedule.

I hear it said that a government agency can't be in the business of producing music, theater and dance performances. That's naïve. The government has long since become a sponsor and consumer of performances and art, and some reconciliation is needed. In the meantime, we go on and produce a season of events that will bring life and relevance to great museums with national treasures. Cynthia and the Education Services staff have recordings to produce; Martin Williams and Peggy Martin have jazz concerts and publications to produce, Peggy, Sharyn Reitz and Cindy Hutchins have innovative musical theater programs to put on the stage. Bernice Reagon has research and performances of gospel and spiritual songs to organize; Jim Weaver has concerts of three centuries of chamber music to produce and the Discovery Theater has children waiting to discover the wonders of life and art.

Not everything works. A planned exploration of American comedy traditions is to begin with a performance by Mort Sahl. The Castle fears he's too political, and his performance is cancelled. I'm also urged to put aside critical study and performances of rock and roll and other modern musical developments. The Kennedy Center has suggested collaboration on a music festival, but we can't work with their schedule.

But Brock Holmes, Jim Weaver and I re-create a concert that might have been given by the Hutchinson Family Singers. They were America's most popular entertainers, circa 1840 – 1860. Putting the program together is a challenge. We're employing theater skills to interpret music history. Four talented singers, accompanied by period instruments, perform political songs, comedy songs, nostalgic songs, abolitionist hymns – the concert is staged in the Renwick Gallery and recorded. Ernestine Perrie comes in to direct.

Martin continues to produce albums devoted to the compositions of Duke Ellington. His arguments, supporting his contention that Ellington is a major American composer, are strong and well reasoned.

Research and reconstruction of original musical theater productions continues. My goal here is to interpret musical theater works within the context of their time and their relevance to the evolution of an American art form. Frank Kermode, the great literary critic and Norton professor at Harvard, provides some reasons. "Interpretation protects the works of the past from becoming disposable junk by astonishing the readers, making them take a second look. It keeps the past alive." I hope our reconstructions of American musicals will astonish listeners and make them take a second look. The first venture is a reconstruction of the 1910 hit, *Naughty Marietta*, Victor Herbert's most successful operetta. We have produced an archival album of previously recorded Herbert performances. Now we can examine his use of dance and style history, his orchestration assistance for a young George Gershwin, and acknowledge his role in creating fair business practices for theater writers and composers. I conduct the orchestra, chorus and soloists and the *New Yorker Magazine* critic writes about the recording "it's excellent... a revelation. Herbert is a principle founder of our musical theater....lovely melodies, masterful orchestration." He says my direction is 'very precise.' It's the first recording of Herbert's score. The only remaining copy is Herbert's hand-written original lodged in the Library of Congress. I try and follow Herbert's markings and directions to the letter. I've cast Judy Blazer, a talented young singing actress, in the title role. "She stands out!" writes the critic.

Naughty Marietta was originally produced by Oscar Hammerstein, grandfather of the Oscar Hammerstein II, who would later give the musical stage such hits as *Oklahoma*, *Carousel* and *South Pacific*. The production cost more than $75,000, a large sum for the period, but a small fraction of the cost of musicals in Oscar II's era. Emma Trentini, the original *Marietta*, had been a star in Hammerstein's Manhattan Opera House, and she was paid the unusually high weekly fee of $750. Ticket prices ranged from twenty-five cents to two dollars. Herbert received a weekly royalty of three percent of the gross receipts, plus royalties from sheet music and phonograph records. After 136 performances in New York, the company went on Boston where the show continued for the season, then moved to Chicago.

scene from Naughty Marietta, Elvira Green, Wayne Turnage, Leslie Harrington, Judy Blazer, Joseph deGenova - the Catholic University of Am. A Cappella Choir, Maureen Codelka-conductor

scene from Naughty Marietta, Judy Blazer, Leslie Harrington

James Morris, conductor

Bernice Reagon heads our Black Culture Program, and she produces a multi-disk recording, *Voices of the Civil Rights Movement*. It's a documentary in sound, where Bernice explores the vital role music played in the civil rights movement of the 1950's and '60's.

183

Voices of the Civil Rights Movement

The civil rights movement hasn't been touched by museum historians. For the recording, Bernice uses archival resources, commercial and field recordings to assemble a moving history of mass meetings, ensembles and songleaders.

Meanwhile, Ripley is adding to his remarkable record of acquisitions and expansions. But acquiring and exhibiting is expensive, and I hear about new strategies for financial re-alignment and fund raising.

Thanks to collector Warren Robbins and some devoted allies, there's going to be a Museum of African Art! And the vast Asian art collections of Arthur Sackler, together with the

184

papers of Henri Vever, are being added to the holdings of the Freer Gallery. New space must be found for housing and exhibition.

Is there space for another building on the Mall? It will be difficult to come by. So the gardens and parking lots near the Castle are dug up, and new buildings constructed - underground.

We issue the *Smithsonian Collection of Country Music*, a multi-disk set of recordings that follows the development and growing popularity of American country music. It traces the emergence of a popular culture genre and follows its journey from down-home entertainment to the musical mainstream. And Harold Closter plans a series of country music concerts that compliments the recorded package.

And Julian Euell calls our staff together, and presents me with the Smithsonian Outstanding Performance Award.

We publish a series of recordings by the 20th Century Consort that include contemporary compositions by Stephen Albert, George Crumb, Mario Davidovsky, Joseph Schwantner, Maurice Wright and others. With these recordings we can show important, present-day American contributions to the world of music. I'm asked by the National Endowment for the Arts to consult on the use of recordings to promote interest in American music, and I'm happy to respond.

Now there's talk of cutting funds for our programs, and re-programming the money. But canceling performances disrupts audience building. Chamber music programs, particularly those using the instrument collection, are a priority. Jazz and popular culture programs have strong advocates. The Discovery Theater is self-supporting, even making a profit. The contemporary music programs? They are enjoyed by a small audience, but have few out-spoken advocates. And they are expensive. So, in spite of my grand statements about the museum's important role in presenting new music, I reluctantly decided to cut the Hirshhorn concerts by the 20th Century Consort. The Consort leaders appeal to Congressman Sidney Yates, chair of the Smithsonian appropriations committee. Yates likes our programs - understands the plight of contemporary music – and opposes cuts. Included with Yates' response is a request that I appear, with other bureau heads, at the next budget hearings. I believe Yates' request signals an increased appropriation.

All the while I'm reminded that the Smithsonian can be a colorful and quixotic place. Lavish receptions under the huge east-Indian shamiana on the museum roof terrace. A tall, balding scholar arrives at work in drag, but no one notices a curator in camisole. An executive is chauffeured to and from work to avoid drunken collisions in the parking lot. A disgruntled employee leaves a basket of dung under the tail of the Natural History Museum's giant elephant. The clean-up crew says, "its not my job." Call the zoo to get the poo. And the recurring question? Is John Dillinger's preserved penis really among the Smithsonian's collection of historic artifacts?

Word from the Castle says that earned income will now flow directly to the general fund. Four years earlier I argued against it, saying that income derived from the talents of artists should be used to gain exposure for other artists. This time I risk losing the argument. An appropriation from Yates would off-set the risk.

A fierce competition for money is a regular Smithsonian exercise. It's difficult to access one's place in Ripley's hierarchy. He occasionally suggests 'closing out' or 'spinning off' a program or a bureau. Is he serious when he suggests 'spinning off' the Folklife Festival to the National Park Service or 'spinning off' the jazz program to the Kennedy Center? Are programs so expendable? Is your office or bureau expendable? Is it a game of 'flinch?' To those who are deeply invested, it's a debilitating experience.

We begin a more didactic approach to re-issued jazz recordings. Martin compiles a thought-provoking two-disk album that traces John Birks "Dizzy" Gillespie's development as soloist and sometime composer-orchestrator.

Shirley Cherkasky had managed the Folklife Festival's *Old Ways in the new World* program with skill and efficiency. Now she became our liaison with the Smithsonian museums. Gradually, our original mission – was being accomplished. Some of our initiatives took root. Museum directors saw attendance increase, the press showed more interest and education programs received more support. Shirley also coordinated our on-going struggles to establish a dance program, and with Sali Ann Kreigsman produced lectures and workshops featuring Charles (Honi) Coles, Edward Villella and others.

As time passed I saw some buy-in to enlivenment ideas by curators and administrators. I also saw an emerging need for ownership of these ideas, and a desire by museum professionals to create their own enlivenment initiatives. And

187

indeed, the new National Museum of African American History and Culture has its own performing arts program director.

Shirley was very effective in creating holiday programs that explored the traditions and cultural history of holiday celebrations and brought new, delighted crowds to the American History museum. Indeed, it occurred to me that Ripley's strategy may have been to use the Division of Performing Arts as a prod to museum directors to become more proactive. Such a strategy would account for his lack of enthusiasm and support for jazz and popular culture programs.

Dizzy Gilllespie, The Development of an American Artist

The recording follows Gillespie's artistic development and I'm devoted to the idea that our educational efforts may demonstrate an artist's growth. And I hope the recording will serve as a guide for similar recordings.

A very nice recognition of our work comes when the New York Times carries a feature story that says, "The Smithsonian, with its musical research and recordings, and it's inventive performances, in now the closest thing the country has to a Ministry of Culture," Sweet words.

American Musical Theater programs delve into the history and performance styles of vaudeville - the start of American entertainment as big business.

Cook & Brown of the Copasetics,
Ernest (Brownie) Brown, Charles Cook

We recall the essence of vaudeville, the acts, the song and dance, the comedy sketches, the ventriloquists, the acrobats, the animal and specialty acts. It was vaudeville that witnessed the transformation of American entertainment into a big business. Ernestine Perrie is contracted to research and direct. We find still-living vaudevillians like dancer Hal Le Roy and comic Sid Stone, and bring them to our stage. Joe Silver, the gravel-voiced Broadway and film actor, joins film and television veteran Paul Dooley to re-construct classic comedy sketches. The vaudeville show is very popular with our audience – a big hit. I call Roger Stevens at the Kennedy Center and suggest Broadway revival possibilities. Stevens likes the idea, and sends me to New York to talk with his partner, Robert Whitehead. Alas, illness delays progress, and finally makes the revival idea impossible.

The theater moves on, and we follow, exploring the wit and wisdom of the musical comedies and revues.

scene from The Revue in America, Gene Johnson, Muareen Ribble

In another venture in musical theater research, we produce scenes from ragtime-era shows. Max Morath heads the cast, with period dances reconstructed by Lee Theodor and her American Dance Machine. The 'Machine' collects the history of musical theater choreography, the work of Jack Cole, Bob Fosse, Gwen Verdon, Jerome Robbins, Michael Kidd and others. Surely this kind of collecting is a museum function, but where can we house such a collection? I write a script for a Dance Machine performance on CBS-TV, and hope to aid Theodor's efforts to save the record of creative dance works from obscurity.

Our musical theater programs examine the career of Kurt Weill. With theater revolutionary Bertolt Brecht, Weill creates a new style of musical theater in Germany. But Weill is a Jew, and he flees to America, and with collaborators like Paul Green and Ira Gershwin, finds an American voice. We created a living exhibition of Weill's work, a musical biography that reached from Berlin to Paris to North Carolina to New York.

scene from Kurt Weill, a Musical Biography,
Barbabra McCulloh, Richard Estes

In 1982 I am promoted to the Senior Executive Service. Secretary Ripley calls and offers congratulations.

Roger Kennedy is appointed Director of the National Museum of American History. He calls for assistance. Doubleday Publishing has underwritten a series of prestige lectures, and Kennedy needs help with subjects and speakers. Martin suggests Gunther Schuller, composer, scholar and President of the New England Conservatory of Music to speak on Sarah Vaughn's mastery as a beyond-category singer. No one would argue about Vaughn's preeminence, and I agree to produce the event. Lengthy negotiations follow, with calls to

Vaughn's unresponsive agents, calls to Schuller, and more calls to Vaughn's management. No response. Time passes. Kennedy holds the purse strings, and he gets antsy at the slow negotiations. Tensions build. Someone suggests I call record and concert producer Norman Ganz for help. Ganz suggests I telephone Vaughn directly, and gives me her unlisted phone number. I call and leave a message. I'm in the conference room when that wonderful assistant, Mary Steward runs in. "Sarah Vaughn's on the phone," an out-of-breath Mary says. On the phone, Vaughn is apologetic and exceedingly polite, and says she never received my messages. She agrees to the booking.

A large crowd of invited guests are gathered in the National Museum of American History's Flag Hall. In the background, the original Star Spangled Banner is displayed. In the foreground is the visitor's escalator, and a platform with a piano. Schuller speaks, remembering and praising previous Vaughn performances and recordings. As he comes to the end of his remarks, Vaughn rides into view on the escalator, steps onto the platform and sings for 40 minutes. The audience is ecstatic. So is Kennedy. And so am I.

Another Doubleday lecture, and I suggest John Houseman as lecturer. In Ripley's mind he's still associated with the errant Sound and Light project. But he's had a noteworthy life, as mechanic and mover, as Romanian-born war refugee, commodities broker, bon vivant, stage director, friend of George Gershwin, and partner of Orson Welles in Federal Theater projects. He was also the producer of the much praised *Citizen Kane* and other films. I make cuttings from his published autobiography. He seems surprised that the

193

cuttings work so well. We agree I will produce. We secure the permission of composer Virgil Thomson to excerpt parts of his opera *Four Saints in Three Acts,* with text by Gertrude Stein (she who wrote 'A Rose is a Rose'). Houseman was the original *Four Saints* director. The event plays to standing room only in American History's flag hall. The Howard University chorus, three excellent soloists, a pianist and Houseman turn in an unforgettable performance.

John Houseman never passes up a good idea. When we shelved the Sound and Light idea, he taught acting at the Juilliard School, with Patti LuPone and Kevin Kline among the first graduates. Then he founds The Acting Company, a touring ensemble. Now Houseman takes my script, makes a few changes and produces it as a touring show for the Company. He somehow forgets to give me credit for the show, but invites me to the opening performance. I'm unable to attend.

The Doubleday Lectures, with their elite corporate and society audiences, glamorous catered receptions, and focus on celebrity, are not aimed at the broader public I have been asked to reach. They seem a far cry from democratizing and enlivening the museums, but Smithsonian officialdom seem very pleased with this use of my talents and experience. At times, it's hard to keep your head on straight.

Our work has generated attention in a national community of artists. We have developed a reputation for caring about social issues, and we've included ideals in our plans. That leads to artists who want to work with us, want collaboration. Some of them bring us projects to consider. On

194

such is stage and film actor Herschel Bernardi, TV star of *Hail to the Chief, Seventh Avenue, Arnie* – Broadway star of *,Zorba,* and *Fiddler on the Roof.* He wants to pay deserved tribute to the Yiddish theater of his youth. We begin collaboration on a theater piece about the 1920's and '30's, the crowded tenements, the poverty, the theater, Yiddish life and the culture of New York City's lower east side. Bernardi's illness prevents the projects completion.

Designer and author Edwin Schlossberg proposes construction of a huge model of the human body, to be installed on the Mall. He's previously designed a unique children's museum in Brooklyn. His Smithsonian plan calls for children to move through the interior of the body model, playing while they learn the intricate systems of circulation. The idea is intriguing, complicated and expensive. After months of consideration the proposal is shelved, and he moves on – ultimately to marry Carolyn Kennedy.

Famed British stage and film director Peter Brook is developing a stage production based on the anthropological study of an African tribe that faces extinction. Brook has an international theater reputation. His creative stage adaptation of *The Persecution and Assassination of Jean Paul Marat as Performed by the Inmates of the Asylum at Charenton Under the Direction of the Marquis de Sade,* (the title usually reduced to *Marat / Sade,*) is an international hit. His revolutionary production of Shakespeare's *Midsummer Night's Dream,* for the Royal Shakespeare Company, draws capacity audiences wherever it plays, and assures Brook's listing among the world's theater leadership. He's thinking of producing the African play in a non-traditional location, possibly a museum environment. I immediately think of the stale African ethnology exhibit in the National Museum of Natural History. Brook invites me fly to London, to see a preview, then to Paris to consult about a Smithsonian performance. Stimulating discussions. Alas, after lengthy investigations, I determine there's no appropriate space in any Smithsonian museum.

In all our work, we endeavor to waken the viewer, to stimulate a sense of wonder. I see our job as finding ways for information to come through to an audience, to find higher forms of truth, to communicate through involvement.

And in all the work, all the proposals, all the ideas, we're aided and supported by a marvelous boss. Assistant Secretary Julian Euell loves music, understands its role in the history of American culture and appreciates the creativity of the musicians that give it life. He is a child of Harlem, a gifted jazz musician and protégé of Charles Mingus. Before the Smithsonian, he was an associate of psychologist and educator Kenneth Clark, the scholar and sociologist who defined the harmful effects of segregated schools.

Somehow, in this period, I made time for personal things. In 1979 I married Cynthia Ann Hamra Hightower. She has been my faithful and loving companion. Her love, support, energy, creativity, good taste and resourcefulness has improved my life and sustained me in good times and bad.

As to what happened with the American College Theater Festival, it's now a program of the Kennedy Center for the Performing Arts, with annual presentations that involve more than 600 academic institutions nationwide and engages more than 18,000 students. I fondly remember 'Mama,' dear Peggy Wood, and hope she would be pleased with the outcome. And the carousel is still turning.

I'm proud of our accomplishments. I'm thankful that earned income from our recording business has paid for much of it. And I'm a bit resentful that the Smithsonian has not been more forthcoming in support. Now I want to pursue new ventures in music, in theater research and production, wishing all the while for an adequate theater with seating capacity that would produce reasonable revenues. I would like to work on a history of film and television, and produce some revolutionary performances. I would like to study performance practices in all periods of music and theater. I would like to look at the history of rock and roll and rap and hip-hop and whatever comes next. And I often think about Franz Schubert and his great musical legacy - the 600 or so wonderful songs – many of which were performed in informal, house concert settings. I would like to create informal, house concert venues where the great American Song Book will be performed by artists with taste and intelligence, a place for recognizing the past, and hopefully the future genius of American songwriters.

With the help of a strong, energetic staff, we've done some damn good work. A bright young popular culture scholar, Dwight Bowers, joins the staff and his knowledge and point of view adds depth to our programs. In 1984, J.R. Taylor wins a Grammy Award for *Big Band Jazz* - Best Historic Album. Salli Ann Kriegsman brings experience and a keen mind to an exploration of American dance. And Bernice Reagon continues her seminal research in black culture.

For some time I have struggled to find a method for measuring the value of performing arts to museum or cultural institutions. Value is a slippery concept. So is scholarship, but the academic world has agreed that peer review will suffice. No such agreement exists within the performing arts. I can see that our work has been useful as a change agent, an agent provocateur. We have led, provoked, and sometimes agitated the established museums to abandon their complacency and challenge viewers. But enthusiasm for change can be trampled in the scurry to comply, to avoid conflict. And as I write, the Smithsonian tries to salvage some credibility lost by removing a video from the National Portrait Gallery's "Hide/Seek" exhibition. The institution fared better when performing arts programs were used to remedy racial and social bias,

During this period, the Smithsonian Collection of Recordings continues to grow, and to sell; from 9 recordings with sales of $150,000 in 1977 to more than 50 recordings with sales of $5,800,000 in 1982. Income from recording sales pay for most of the museum programs we produce. In 1983, with the introduction of new technologies and products, the record industry experiences one of its periodic decline and our recording sales follow the trend and also decline. As a result, there was a change in Smithsonian accounting policy. From its inception, record production costs had been expensed over a three year period, reflecting the assumed sales life of each recording. With the changing policy, all production costs, past and present, were expensed in one year. The result is a substantial loss to the Division of Performing Arts bottom line. I protest the accounting change, pointing out that no allowance is made for accumulated assets and continued income. My arguments did not prevail, but in fact, the Smithsonian Collection of Recording continue to sell for several years.

I had served a year in the WWII-era U. S. Navy, two years in the Korea-era U. S. Army, and several years in the peace-time National Guard and at the U. S. Department of Commerce. Together with my eighteen years at the Smithsonian, I had accumulated 25 years of government service and am eligible for retirement. I decided to leave Government service in 1984. Before retirement I annotate a major record publication; *American Popular Song: Six Decades of Songwriters and Singers.* My collaborators are J. R. Taylor and Dwight Bowers. The publication is nominated for a Grammy Award for Best Historic Album and produces substantial revenue for the Smithsonian. Also in 1984, the Division of Performing Arts is officially disbanded, with Federal Employees transferred to the National Museum of American History and Trust Fund employees transferred to the Resident Associates Program.

On retirement, I partner with famed sports-caster Jim Simpson and form The Production Group, Inc. to produce recordings, commercial television, training videos, video documentaries and films. I also continue to write, produce and direct stage and video productions, and to teach. When the press questions Secretary Ripley about the reason for my retirement, his comment is, "Jim Morris is a free spirit."

Epilogue

In 1983, Cynthia Hightower left the Smithsonian to become Director of the Arts and Culture Programs/Educational Branch, at the National Archives and Records Administration.

From 1988 to 1990 I taught singing to deaf and hearing impaired students at Gallaudet University, developing written materials, imaging, touch, audio feedback and oscilloscope technology in an effort to bridge the gap between real and imagined vocal sounds. Teaching music performance to the hearing challenged was an idea of Diane Merchant Loomis, director of the University Music Program for Deaf and Hard of Hearing students at Gallaudet. It was a truly revolutionary idea. Diane Loomis now holds a doctorate degree in education. She was a singer and pianist who lost much of her hearing as a result of a college-age illness. She remains a bright, intelligent scholar, a caring teacher and a passionate advocate for the hearing impaired.

S. Dillon Ripley retired as Secretary of the Smithsonian Institution in 1984. He was a man of great energy and intelligence who revolutionized the Smithsonian, added new museums and programs and opened new avenues of research and presentation. On his retirement he was awarded the Presidential Medal of Freedom, the United States' highest civilian award. He died in 2001 from a heart ailment.

In 1983, Julian Euell left the Smithsonian to become director of the Oakland (California) Museum of History and Science. From 1991 to 1995 he was director of Louis Armstrong House in Brooklyn, New York. Prior to his Smithsonian tenure as assistant secretary for public service he was a respected jazz musician, and in the 1990s he returned to performing.

In 1996 I wrote and directed *In The Mood*, a revue about the music of the World War II era. I believe the show reminded audiences that in the darkness of a long and terrible war, American songwriters sustained the nation's spirit with an out-pouring of marvelous song.

**In the Mood, a WWII Musical Revue, Left to Right,
Ann Johnson, Cindy Hutchins, Brenda Brody, Brian Donnelly
String of Pearls Orchestra-with Bud Forrest photographed
on the steps of the National Archives**

The revue premiered at the National Archives and Records Administration, part of a celebration of the 50th Anniversary of WWII. Responding to a huge public demand, a follow-up performance was staged on Constitution Avenue, on the steps of the Archives. *In the Mood* was designated Official Commemorative Show for WWII by the USO, and subsequently toured the United States and Europe.

In 1983 Martin Williams joined the Smithsonian Press and completes previously begun work on a four volume collection of George Gershwin's music for the stage and screen, the concert hall, for popular song and for jazz. W.K. McNeil completed *The Blues, a Smithsonian Collection of Classic Blues Singers*. Martin also annotated *The*

203

Smithsonian Collection of Big Band Jazz which earned him a Grammy Award. During his Smithsonian tenure Martin authored numerous books and articles on American popular culture. He retired in 1991 and died in 1992 of complication from cancer.

In 1982 Ralph Rinzler founded the Center for Folklife and Cultural Heritage. He was instrumental in the Smithsonian's acquisition of the Folkways Recording Archive. He was appointed Assistant Secretary for Public Service in 1983 and returned to the Center in 1986. He died in 1994 following a long illness. The cause of death was not reported. Program concepts for the Smithsonian Folklife Festival have continued to evolve, and the Smithsonian will present the 44th Festival in 2011.

From 1985 to 1988, Dr. Bernice Johnson Reagon was head of the Program in Black American Culture at the National Museum of American History. In 1989, Bernice was awarded a MacArthur Fellowship (known as the 'genius grant') for her contributions to the field of Black music and culture.

From 1985 to 1995, The Production Group, Inc. produced numerous films, recordings, television documentaries and videos, sponsored by organizations that included Abbott Labs, AT&T, Westinghouse Corporation, SAS, the National School Boards Association, the City of Alexandria and others

In 1990, Congress appropriated funds for a Jazz Masterworks Orchestra in recognition of the importance of

jazz in American culture. David N. Baker, a renowned educator, composer, performer, author and conductor is the orchestra's artistic director. The mission of the orchestra is to present and preserve the legacy of jazz.

In the 1990's, the National Museum of American History appointed John Hasse, Curator, Division of Culture and the Arts. Hasse then became the founder and co-director of the Jazz Masterworks Orchestra and founder of America's Jazz Heritage, a partnership with the Lila Wallace-Readers Digest Fund.

Dwight Blocker Bowers continues to produce recordings and add to the collections of the National Museum of American History. In 1996 he was the joint-organizer of the National Portrait Gallery exhibition, *Red, Hot and Blue- A Salute to American Musicals*. His other exhibition subjects include Duke Ellington, Ella Fitzgerald, Irving Berlin and *American Musicals at the Drury Lane*. He is currently Curator, Division of Culture and the Arts, National Museum of American History. Dwight also initiated an excellent series of American Song programs, utilizing first-rate singers under the musical direction of Howard Breitbart. The series was very popular with audiences and should be a regular offering of the National Museum of American History.

The Smithsonian Chamber Orchestra,
Kenneth Slowik, conductor

The Smithsonian Chamber Music Society, originally led by James Weaver and now directed by Kenneth Slowik, continues to reach international audiences through recordings, broadcasts and tours. With Slowik's creative leadership, the orchestra has reached a very high level of musical performance. The Society continues to produce some 30 concerts each year, and the Smithsonian remains the only museum in the world with an active and long-term program using musical instruments as they were intended by their makers.

Beginning circa 2000 James Weaver led an effort to establish The National Music Center and Museum, with three performance spaces including a 3500 seat auditorium.

Initially unrealized, the project is now a key element in the newly revitalized waterfront in Washington, D.C.

In 2009 I was named a Smithsonian Legacy Honoree by the Center for Folklife and Cultural Heritage.

Also in 2009 I was given a Community Builders Award by the Grand Lodge of Masons of the Commonwealth of Virginia.

END

Index

Made in the USA
Middletown, DE
11 July 2020

12456868R00129